The Pattern of Our Days

Worship in the Celtic Tradition from the Iona Community

The Iona Community
Edited by Kathy Galloway

PAULIST PRESS
New York/Mahwah, N.J.

The publisher gratefully acknowledges the use of the following: Scripture quotations marked (TEV) are from Today's English Version—Second Edition © 1992 by American Bible Society. Used by permission. "Go forth into the world in peace" from *The Prayer Book as Proposed in 1928,* copyright © The Central Board of Finance of the Church of England, reproduced by permission. Excerpt from *George MacLeod* by Ron Ferguson, © 1992 by HarperCollins Publishers. Reprinted by permission of HarperCollins Publishers, London, England. Prayer by Edmund S. P. Jones, reproduced by permission of Stainer & Bell, Ltd., London, England. Material from *Threshold of Light,* edited by A. M. Alchin and Esther de Waal, copyright © 1986 by A. M. Alchin and Esther de Waal. Published by Templegate Publishers, Springfield, Illinois. Used with permission. "Home," "Exile" and "Promised Land," © 1996 Wild Goose Resource Group, Iona Community. Used by permission. Material from *Book of a Thousand Prayers* edited by Angela Ashwin. Used by permission of HarperCollins Publishers Ltd. Material from *The Book of Common Worship,* © 1993 Westminster John Knox Press. Used by permission of Westminster John Knox Press.

This edition of *The Pattern of Our Days* is published by arrangement with Wild Goose Publications, The Iona Community, 840 Govan Road, Glasgow, Scotland. The Authors have asserted their right under the Copyright, Designs and Patents Act, 1988, to be identified as the Authors of this Work.

Cover design by Cynthia Dunne

Illustrations © Adrienne Kern

Copyright © 1996 by The Authors

Library of Congress Cataloging-in-Publication Data

The pattern of our days : worship in the Celtic tradition from the Iona Community / the Iona Community ; edited by Kathy Galloway.
    p. cm.
   ISBN 0-8091-3860-3 (alk. paper)
   1. Prayers. 2. Worship programs. 3. Iona Community—Prayer books and devotions—English. I. Galloway, Kathy. II. Iona Community.
BV245.P33   1999
264—dc21
                                       98-56177
                                         CIP

Published by Paulist Press
997 Macarthur Boulevard
Mahwah, New Jersey 07430

www.paulistpress.com

Printed and bound in the
United States of America

The Iona Community

The Iona Community is an ecumenical Christian community, founded in 1938 by the late George MacLeod (Very Rev. Lord MacLeod of Fuinary). Gathered around the rebuilding of the ancient monastic buildings of Iona Abbey, but with its original inspiration in the poorest areas of Glasgow during the Depression, the Iona Community has sought ever since the "rebuilding of the common life," bringing together work and worship, prayer and politics, the sacred and the secular in an incarnational faith.

The Iona Community today is a movement of around 200 members, 1,200 associate members, and 2,000 friends. The members—women and men from many backgrounds, countries, and denominations—are committed to a rule of daily prayer and Bible reading, sharing and accounting for their use of time and money, regular meeting, and action for justice and peace.

The Iona Community maintains three centers on Iona and Mull: Iona Abbey and the MacLeod Centre on Iona, and Camas Adventure Camp on the Ross of Mull. Its base is in Community House, Glasgow, where it also supports work with young people, the Wild Goose Worship and Resource Groups, and a publishing house, Wild Goose Publications. It publishes a bimonthly magazine, *Coracle*.

The Worship of the Iona Community

Worship has been fundamental to the life of the Iona Community since it began. It was with the intention of breaking down the barriers between our everyday lives and language and the life of the worshipping community that the first members, ministers and craftsmen engaged together in the rebuilding of the Abbey ruins, began and ended each day with common worship. Work and recreation were encompassed within the pattern of worship because they are not to be held apart. Each informs the other.

The pattern remains the same still on Iona. The continuing group on whose life the daily worship is based is the resident community living in the Iona Abbey and the MacLeod Centre. Their work and that of the guests in the centers is rooted in worship. We are accountable in all things to God. We make account as a community in our worship. In the mornings the worship is the daily service of the Iona Community during which the members are prayed for by name. Evening worship reflects the concerns of the Iona Community, which are, of course, concerns of the whole Christian community: justice and peace, healing, creation, commitment, community, and celebration.

At Camas too the day is encompassed by worship, either held in the Chapel of the Nets or outside on the rocks by the water. Camas worship, in the remote and intimate setting of interdependency and dependency on nature, offers unique opportunities for creative worship.

But the worship of the Iona Community does not take place only on Iona. There are many occasions when the community gathers on the mainland—in the Family Groups, which are its base communities; in plenary session in different places; for special events and acts of witness. And each individual member is committed to working out the rule of the community in her or his own context of place, work, people, and worshipping community. Therefore, there are many occasions and situations in which the community is engaged in finding "new ways to touch the hearts of all" in worship on the mainland.

Because the members of the Iona Community (and its associate members, friends, and staff) come from such a diversity of background, place, faith tradition, and experience, the kinds of worship they are involved in are enormously varied. The life and service of the local church, the work of community and campaigning groups, ecumenical and international events, small groups and house churches—all are part of the engagement of members. All of these are proper places for prayer.

But whether on Iona or at Camas or on the mainland, whether it is the community gathered or the community dispersed, some features of our worship are constant.

It is *incarnational.* At its heart is the belief that God in Jesus Christ became a human being like us, sharing fully in all the hopes and fears, joys and sorrows of our lives, to let us know that God loves us, forgives us, makes us whole, and desires to give us life in all its fullness. Therefore we believe that there is no part of life that is beyond the reach of our faith. The word of life is as much for our politics as for our prayers.

It is *historical.* It draws on the experience and creativity of our mothers and fathers in the faith. The Celtic church of

Columba had a strong and deep sense of the incarnation and of the glory of God in creation. We share these beliefs in both the incarnation and the integrity of creation, and they find expression in our worship. We value the Benedictine traditions of hospitality and the centrality of prayer (though we may go about these in very different ways). We drink deeply from the well of biblical faith of our Reformed forbears. Sometimes we use orders and liturgies that have come down through the ages. They are part of the great drama of worship. They also remind us that we are part of a worldwide church.

It is *ecumenical* because we are an ecumenical community and part of a worldwide church. We are constantly receiving gifts from the various traditions represented in our membership—from Quaker and Anglican, Methodist and Baptist, Presbyterian and Roman Catholic. We cannot but be ecumenical. We do not believe this condemns us to the blandness of the lowest common denominator. We believe this challenges us to be open, honest, and creative. This, of course, is a constant struggle, and sometimes it is a source of conflict and pain. But these are the places we grow.

To be ecumenical in its true sense demands that we be *inclusive.* We believe that God welcomes everyone who seeks to worship in spirit and in truth. So it is a matter of faithfulness to God's purposes that we make sure people do not feel unwelcome by the use of language that excludes on account of gender, race, or culture. Nor should our worship only be understood by people who have degrees in theology or who have grown up in the church. It also means that planning and leadership of worship are not confined to the clergy. Since liturgy is the work of the people, we should not accept this merely as a pious phrase but should make it live, so that the people are fully and actively engaged in worship in songs, responses, and open prayer; in symbolic acts; and in the many ways in which it is possible to "break the Word" in order that it may be shared.

And, finally, our worship is *creaturely.* We are whole people, God's creation, and we want to respond through our senses as well as our intellects. In movement and stillness, through touch and sight and sound, through smell and taste, we are gifted with many ways to pray.

Prayer changes people. Faith changes people. This we believe. Therefore, we try to be *open to change,* to the new, in our worship. God meets us out there on the borders as much as in what is familiar and reassuring.

The Iona Community has been blessed in recent years by the existence and contribution of the Wild Goose Worship and Resource Groups. Their songs, liturgical pieces, drama, and meditations have found recognition, acceptance, and widespread gratitude. Because we as a community have profited so greatly from the work of the Resource Groups and have had so much access to their creativity, it is sometimes easy to take it for granted. This we do not want to do. It has given us "a new song to sing." It has introduced us to the wealth of ways in which the church throughout the world sings its faith, especially the church in the poorest countries of the world.

The material in this book reflects the faith and engagement of a community that has nurtured both for its members. We offer it in the hope that it may yield good fruits to those who use it.

This book has been a common task. The editorial group has approached it as a labor of love. My thanks to them: Joanna Anderson, Ruth Burgess, Malcolm King, Cilla McKenna, Kate McIlhagga.

Kathy Galloway
Community House, Glasgow

Foreword

Worship has always been at the heart of the life of the Iona Community. It is the mainspring of all our activities and both the beginning and the end of our commitment to world peace, social justice, and the rediscovery of an integrated spirituality. We are proud of the publications we have already been producing as resources for the worship of the wider church—the prayers of George MacLeod, succeeding editions of Abbey Worship Books, and the wide range of material produced through the creativity of John Bell, Graham Maule, and their colleagues on the Wild Goose Resource and Worship Groups.

For some years there has been a feeling within the Iona Community that we should find an opportunity to complement these by bringing together some of the material produced by members of the community. Community members work and worship in a wide variety of local situations and are involved, whether ordained or lay, in many different worship settings. This book reflects the strength and breadth of the community's commitment to forms of worship that are inclusive, accessible, and rooted in a context of engagement with the life needs and problems of the world. I believe that it will be welcomed and well used among all those throughout Britain and beyond whose support and interest the community values so much and which I have particularly appreciated since becoming Leader. With our present membership and the degree of involvement I know exists in developing creative approaches to worship that are appropriate to particular local circumstances, I believe that we as a community have the capacity to produce several companion volumes to this one, and I look forward to their publication in the years ahead!

These are challenging times for the church and exciting times for the Iona Community. Changes continue on mainland and island. The millennium approaches, and before that, important political and social events will involve both the community and individual members. Kathy Galloway and those who have worked with her are to be congratulated on producing this book. I hope that everyone who uses the liturgies and resources in it will find their faith enhanced and their worship enriched.

Norman Shanks
Leader of the Iona Community

Using the Book

The first section of the book, **Liturgies,** consists of a number of complete liturgies organized under four headings, representing important subjects or concerns in the life of the Iona Community. There is a short introduction to these at the beginning of each heading.

The liturgies can be used complete as they stand with appropriate amendment and additions to take note of the local context. Or the shape of the liturgy can be used, but other prayers, readings, and songs may be substituted. Or they can simply be used as a source of ideas for other acts of worship.

The second section, **Resources**, includes prayers, litanies and responses, and a number of readings and meditations. These are arranged, broadly speaking, in a way that reflects the movement of the drama of worship, the great story of salvation, a movement which begins with

- preparation and approach to God, and the recognition and naming of the brokenness of life;
- God's response in the Word, in scripture, in the witness of those who have met the Word in their lives;
- our response to God's liberating Word made flesh in prayer for others, in self-offering, in thanksgiving.

In worship we always begin where we are. In hearing and receiving the Word of life, whether it is one of forgiveness and acceptance, of comfort or challenge, of promise or demand, we are changed. We move to a different place, a place where Jesus is always calling, "Follow me." In this different place we discover, or remember, that we are part of a body, in which "if one part suffers, all the other parts suffer with it; if one part rejoices, all the other parts rejoice with it." We are most fully ourselves when we are most fully part of the body.

Therefore our worship sustains most, refreshes most, has the greatest integrity, not when our words are most beautiful, our liturgies most reverent or innovative, our music most heavenly, but when our lives are most fully engaged. It is important that we do not censor all that we have and all that we are in worship, whether that be feelings, imagination, desire, concern, or the limitations and inadequacy that we sometimes experience. It is better that we make of these an offering. We do not have to be perfect; we do not have to be nice; we only need to know our need of God.

That is not in any way to say that our worship can be slap-dash or ill-prepared. We take care of what we value. If we value the offering of worship, then we want to attend to it with all the care and creativity at our disposal—which is usually much more than we, and sometimes the church, believe.

If this book encourages those who use it to find something more of their own creativity and ability in worship, it will have served its purpose.

Liturgies

Resources

LITURGIES

PILGRIMAGE AND JOURNEYS

Each Wednesday on Iona, the Iona Community invites all those staying on the island, whether in the Abbey, the MacLeod Centre, or elsewhere, to join in a pilgrimage around Iona, visiting places of historical or religious significance and reflecting on our own journeys of faith. On the way we share food, conversation, and silence across barriers of age and experience, language and culture. At each stop, there is a short act of worship.

But pilgrimage is not only something on or to Iona (or indeed to other places of significance for people of faith). Christian faith is often referred to as *the Way* and Christians as *people of the Way.* And indeed, journeys and pilgrimage are powerful human symbols that transcend divisions of religion, culture, history, and geography. Home or origin, departure and destination, travel and homecoming speak a universal human language.

We can conceive of our lives as a journey or pilgrimage, and stages on that journey are marked by ceremony, by rites of passage. But pilgrimage does not need to cover a territory marked out in miles or kilometers. The journey to school or work on the first day may be very long indeed, and some of our most demanding journeys take place in the inner landscape of our lives.

The liturgies in this section relate either to the marking in some way of birth and death (particularly aspects of these that sometimes go unregarded in the worship books of our churches) or to pilgrimages that are not measurable in miles. One of these helps us to look at our local church in a different way. The other remembers the Exodus, the going out of the people of Israel and of Jesus Christ.

1 *The Blessing of Children (Without Baptism)*

Opening responses

Leader: In the beginning, God made the world,
light and dark, shape and void, height and depth,
to tell of love.

ALL: AND GOD SAYS IT IS GOOD.

Leader: In land and sea, in plant and seed,
in growth and decay,
God's love is shown.

ALL: AND GOD SAYS IT IS GOOD.

Leader: In creatures great and creatures small,
in movement and stillness, in birth and death,
God's love is shown.

ALL: AND GOD SAYS IT IS GOOD.

Leader: In woman and man,
in joy and sorrow, in laughter and tears,
God's love is shown.

ALL: AND GOD SAYS IT IS GOOD.

Leader: In the gift of new life, in signs of hope,
in the children we are given,

ALL: GOD'S LOVE IS SHOWN.

Leader: So let us celebrate and give thanks
for the gift of this child/these children.

ALL: WITH GOD WE SAY, "IT IS GOOD."

Leader: Jesus said: Let the children come to me,
do not try to stop them,
for the kingdom of heaven belongs to such as these.

Song

Prayer

Leader: God our Maker,
we praise you for your creation, and especially for life new and renewed. We rejoice and thank you for the life of *(name)* given in love to *(name)* and *(name)* as their child. We pray that *(name)* and *(name)* will, in their loving, guiding, and nurturing of their child, be strengthened and aided by the power and presence of your love in Jesus Christ.
Amen.

Leader: *(Name)* and *(name),* will you, with God's help, strive to share your love, faith, wisdom, and understanding with *(name)* and make for her/him a home where she/he may learn to live in love, peace, and justice?

Caregivers/
Family: We will.

To all others present

Leader: Will you who form the community of love in which *(name)* will grow, keep this child and her/his parents/caregivers in your hearts and prayers, and give an example of faith, hope, and love to them all, with God's help?

ALL: WE WILL

       The parents/caregivers are invited to bless the child first with these words:

Caregivers/
Family: May God's joy be in your heart
       and God's love surround your living.
       Each day and night and
       wherever you roam,
       may you know God's presence.
       In growing and learning,
       in joy and sorrow,
       in friendship,
       in solitude,
       in beginnings and endings,
       may God keep you and bless you
       all the days of your life.
       They kiss the child/ren.
       A candle is handed to the child/ren.

ALL: THE BRIGHT LIGHT OF GOD'S GUARDING
       BE WITH YOU,
       THE BRIGHT LIGHT OF CHRIST'S LOVE
       BE WITH YOU,
       THE BRIGHT LIGHT OF THE SPIRIT'S
       PRESENCE
       SURROUND AND ENFOLD YOU,
       ALL THE DAYS AND NIGHTS OF YOUR LIFE.
       AMEN.

Song

Closing responses

Leader: Making us, shaping us
ALL: BLESSING US, TRUSTING US

Leader:	Leading us, disturbing us
ALL:	EMPOWERING US, LOVING US
Leader:	God of our childhood,
ALL:	GOD OF OUR GROWING,
Leader:	Stay with us on our journey
ALL:	AND BRING US SAFELY HOME.

2 *Liturgy for a Stillborn Child*

As one whom a mother comforts
I will comfort you, says the Lord.
We come here to thank God for *(name of child)*
To thank God for his/her conception,
To thank God for the months she/he
was carried in *(name of mother's)* womb
and in *(name of father's)* heart,
To thank God that in his/her short life
she/he brought joy and laughter,
anticipation and hope for the future.

We gather to share our grief
and our anger that a life promised
has been taken, that hope seems
to have been cut off and joy destroyed.

We are here as *(parent[s], grandparents,*
friends, and family)
to lay our questions,
our sadness, and our hope
at the feet of Christ,

who opened his arms to receive
all who were wounded and distressed.

We have come to acknowledge
our feelings of guilt and failure,
and to affirm our conviction
that death is not the end
but a new beginning.

Jesus says: Those who come to me,
I will not cast out.

*Those present are encouraged to give words to their hopes
and fears, their anger, their sadness; to place flowers,
poems, gifts, symbols of love and light on the coffin or on a
nearby table.*

A time of silence and letting go

Chants
Be still and know / Lord Jesus Christ, Lover of all

Prayer
Said by all:
O God, as *(name of child)*
was cradled in the womb,
cradle her/him and hold her/him
so that as we let her/him go,
we may know that he/she has gone
from our loving presence
into yours forever.
In Jesus' name we pray.
AMEN.

3 | *Liturgy for the Anniversary of a Death*

The setting for this liturgy is some kind of shared gathering, e.g., a family meal, a picnic, a meeting of friends. The physical setting should be relaxed. The liturgy is participative, and leadership should be shared. Take responsibility for each others' feelings. Laughter and tears are appropriate in this setting.

Opening responses

Come among us, God.
You who cast the planets into space
and cradle the sparrow in her nest.
> COME, GOD, AND MEET US HERE.

Come among us, God.
You who bless the poor and the broken
and stand by the sad and the strong.
> COME, GOD, AND MEET US HERE.

Come among us, God.
You who dance in the silence
and shine in the darkness.
> COME, GOD, AND MEET US HERE.

Reading

> *Psalm 139:7–10*

Where shall I go to escape your spirit?
Where shall I flee from your presence?
If I scale the heavens, you are there;
If I lie flat in Sheol, you are there;
If I speed away on the wings of the dawn,
If I dwell beyond the ocean,

Even there your hand will be guiding me,
Your right hand holding me fast.

Revelation 21:3–4
I heard a voice say: Look,
God lives among human beings
and makes a home among them. They are God's people
and God is their God—God is with them.
God will wipe away all tears from their eyes;
there will be no more death and no more
mourning or sadness or pain. The world
of the past has gone.

John 14:1–3
Jesus said: Do not let your hearts be troubled.
You trust in God, trust also in me.
In God's house there are many places to live—
if it were otherwise I would have told you.
I am going now to prepare a place for you,
and after I have gone and prepared you a place,
I shall return to take you to myself,
so that you may be with me, where I am.

A space to remember
*A chance to remember those who have died—to retell stories,
to sing songs, to share common memories, to bring into the
present the things we want to recall, to share silence.*

*Use a ritual action that is meaningful to those present (e.g.,
light a candle, place a stone or flower, float petals in water).
Place something centrally that recalls those who have died.*

All our laughter, all our sadness
SAFE NOW IN GOD'S HANDS

All our anger, all our gladness
SAFE NOW IN GOD'S HANDS

All our stories, all our memories
SAFE NOW IN GOD'S HANDS

Those we remember, those we love
SAFE NOW IN GOD'S HANDS

Sing a song together, listen to some favorite music, have a coffee.

Closing responses
We ask for the love of God
AND THE MESSAGES OF ANGELS

The laughter of Jesus
AND THE STORIES OF THE SAINTS

The power of the Spirit
AND THE STRONG HANDS OF FRIENDS

To bless us on life's journey
AND LEAD US SAFELY HOME.
AMEN.

(From *A Book of a Thousand Prayers,* edited by A. Ashwin, HarperCollins Publishers, 1996.)

Hope and Renewal in Times of Change: Four Exodus Liturgies

*These liturgies are entitled **Home, Exile, Desert, and Promised Land**. These may take place on four consecutive occasions or as one whole act of worship. Thematically, they are appropriate for a number of contexts, since the Exodus journey is a discernable movement in many aspects of human experience, e.g., the passage from childhood through adolescence to maturity, or the stages of community formation.*

It is desirable that people face one another, and that there is a central point where images of each stage are easily visible.

When the four liturgies are taking place as one act of worship, it may be a processing liturgy, somewhat like a Stations of the Cross, whereby the people move from one stage to another, with four points arranged around the room with appropriate images and symbols. During the movement from one stage to another, the following chant may be sung softly:

SEND OUT YOUR LIGHT, LORD,
SEND YOUR TRUTH TO BE MY GUIDE.
THEN LET THEM LEAD ME
TO THE PLACE WHERE YOU RESIDE.

4   HOME

Call to worship

Leader: The Lord says: When the time comes,
I will answer the prayers of my people.

Left: I will betroth you to myself forever
Right: With integrity and justice, with tenderness and love.

Left:	I will betroth you to myself with faithfulness,
Right:	And you will come to know me.

Left:	I will say: You are my people,
Right:	And you will answer: You are our God.

Left:	For once you were outside mercy,
Right:	But now you have been given mercy.

ALL:	THIS IS OUR HOPE, OUR LIVING HOPE. WE SHALL BE GLAD.

Leader:	The Lord says: When the time comes, I will take back my gifts of corn and wine.

Reading
Genesis 18:1–8

Psalm or song
O God, you are my God alone/My Shepherd is the Lord/The love of God comes close/A touching place/Come, host of heaven/Take this moment/May God draw near/Jesus Christ our living Lord

Symbols of home
Suggestions for these might include a bunch of keys, theater masks, toys, or ornaments laid out in a central position so that all are able to see and reflect on them.

Silence to reflect
On the varied meanings that "home" has for each one of us.

A time of witness or exchange about meanings of "home."

Chant

Sung softly and repeatedly

> MAY THE WORDS OF OUR MOUTHS AND THE
> THOUGHTS OF OUR HEARTS
> BE ACCEPTABLE TO YOU,
> GOD OUR STRENGTH AND OUR REDEEMER.
> AMEN. AMEN.

Blessing and repentance

Leader: Strong, sheltering God,
we bless you for all the beautiful things of home:
warmth and shelter when the wind outside is bitter,
food for the body and for the soul,
treasured gifts and treasured memories,
stability, acceptance, care.
We bless you for the chance to be ourselves,
for the tasks that weave the pattern of our days,
for the sweet, familiar round of ordinary things.

ALL: BLESSED ARE YOU, STRONG, SHELTERING GOD.

Leader: But if we have forced unfair expectations on others,
taken their care for granted,
helped to make of a safe place a battleground,
or used our belonging to shut others out,

ALL: HAVE MERCY ON US,
GOD OF FRIEND AND STRANGER.
DISTURB OUR COMPLACENCY,
SHAKE OUR CIRCLES OF CONTENTMENT,
SWEEP THROUGH OUR HEARTS
AND OUR HOUSES

WITH THE NEW BROOM OF YOUR SPIRIT
UNTIL LOVE IS OUR ONLY REFUGE.
AMEN.

Reading
Luke 2:39–52

Prayers of concern
· for all whose homes are places of unhappiness, threat, or insecurity

Chant
LISTEN, LORD. LISTEN, LORD. NOT TO OUR WORDS BUT TO OUR PRAYER. YOU ALONE, YOU ALONE, UNDERSTAND AND CARE.
- · for all whose homes have been broken by family breakdown or by dispossession
- · for all who have no homes

Closing responses
Leader: On our hearts and our houses
ALL: THE BLESSING OF GOD.

Leader: In our coming and going
ALL: THE PEACE OF GOD.

Leader: In our life and believing
ALL: THE LOVE OF GOD.

Leader: At our end and new beginning
ALL: THE ARMS OF GOD TO WELCOME US AND BRING US HOME.
AMEN.[1]

---

[1]© Wild Goose Resource Group, Iona Community.

5 EXILE

Call to worship

Leader: The Lord says: When the time comes, I will answer the prayers of my people.

Left: I will betroth you to myself forever
Right: With integrity and justice, with tenderness and love.

Left: I will betroth you to myself with faithfulness,
Right: And you will come to know me.

Left: I will say: You are my people,
Right: And you will answer: You are our God.

Left: For once you were outside mercy,
Right: But now you have been given mercy.

ALL: THIS IS OUR HOPE, OUR LIVING HOPE. WE SHALL BE GLAD.

Leader: The Lord says: I will fence you in with thorns and build a wall to block the way.

Readings

Genesis 47:1-6; Exodus 1:1-14

Psalm or song

Just as a lost and thirsty deer/Contemporary reproaches/Listen, Lord/Stumbling blocks and stepping stones/Beside the streams of Babylon/The refugees

Symbols of exile

For many people exclusion of various kinds—from work, from political freedoms, from good health, or on the basis of race, gender, or sexuality—may also be experienced as a kind of exile. Suggestions for symbols might include passports, No Entry signs, photographs. People might have been asked in advance to bring a photograph that is dear to them. At the conclusion of the reflection, these might be attached to a board or banner, to be held in prayer.

Silence to reflect

On the varied meanings that "exile" has for each of us.

A Time of Witness or Exchange about meanings of "exile."

Chant

MAY THE WORDS OF OUR MOUTHS...

Blessing and repentance

Leader: God beyond borders,
we bless you for strange places and different dreams,
for the demands and diversity of a wider world,
for the distance that lets us look back and reevaluate,
for new ground where broken stems can take root, grow, and blossom.
We bless you for the friendship of strangers,
the richness of other cultures,
and the painful gift of freedom.

ALL: BLESSED ARE YOU, GOD BEYOND BORDERS.

Leader: But if we have overlooked the exiles in our midst,
heightened their exclusion by our indifference,

given our permission for a climate of fear,
and tolerated a culture of violence,

ALL: HAVE MERCY ON US,
GOD WHO SIDES WITH JUSTICE.
CONFRONT OUR PREJUDICE,
STRETCH OUR NARROWNESS,
SIFT OUT OUR LAWS AND OUR LIVES
WITH THE PENETRATING INSIGHT
OF YOUR SPIRIT
UNTIL GENEROSITY IS OUR ONLY MEASURE.
AMEN.

Reading
Luke 4:16–30

Prayers of concern
· for refugees and political exiles

Chant
LORD JESUS CHRIST, LOVER OF ALL,
TRAIL WIDE THE HEM OF YOUR GARMENT.
BRING HEALING, BRING PEACE.
· for all trapped by their own fear and hostility
· for all who experience exclusion because of poverty,
gender, race, religion

Closing responses
Leader: For all that God can do within us,
For all that God can do without us,
ALL: THANKS BE TO GOD.

Leader: For all in whom Christ lived before us,
For all in whom Christ lives beside us,
ALL: THANKS BE TO GOD.

Leader: For all the Spirit wants to bring us,
For where the Spirit wants to send us,
ALL: THANKS BE TO GOD.

Leader: Listen,
Christ has promised to be with us in the world
as in our worship.
ALL: AMEN, WE GO TO MEET HIM.[2]

6 DESERT

Call to worship

Leader: The Lord says: When the time comes,
I will answer the prayers of my people.

Left: I will betroth you to myself forever
Right: With integrity and justice, with tenderness and love.

Left: I will betroth you to myself with faithfulness,
Right: And you will come to know me.

Left: I will say: You are my people,
Right: And you will answer: You are our God.

Left: For once you were outside mercy,
Right: But now you have been given mercy.

---

[2] Ibid.

ALL: THIS IS OUR HOPE, OUR LIVING HOPE.
WE SHALL BE GLAD.

Leader: The Lord says: I will woo you
and lead you into the wilderness
and speak to your heart.

Readings
Exodus 16:1-6, 35-36, and 17:1-6

Psalm or song
*Lifting my eyes up to the hills/Veni Sancte Spiritus/If you
believe and I believe/The temptations/Come with me, come
wander/The song is love/How long, O Lord/Traveling the
road to freedom*

Symbols of the desert
*Suggestions for these might be stones, sand, weeds, broken
or rusted things. If there is time, people might be invited in
small groups to create desert "gardens" in bowls of sand,
using stones and small pieces of debris. Or people could be
invited to walk silently in a circle, perhaps pausing at "stations," each with a question written on a large sheet: How
long? Where is hope? What shall we pray? Etc. Here they can
pray, light a candle, or write a response.*

Silence to reflect
On the varied meanings that "desert" has for each one of us.
**A time of witness or exchange about meanings of
"desert."**

Chant
MAY THE WORDS OF OUR MOUTHS...

Blessing and repentance

Leader: God of strangeness and desire,
we bless you for enticing us
to the last place we wanted to be,
the place where we can hide no longer,
where we must face our own emptiness
and see our false gods fall.
We bless you for the immeasurable relief
of self-exposure,
for the miracle of survival,
and for coming to us in unexpected guises.

ALL: BLESSED ARE YOU,
GOD OF STRANGENESS AND DESIRE.

Leader: But if we have turned in upon our emptiness,
refused the risks you require of us,
idolized our self-sufficiency,
and clung to our captivity,

ALL: HAVE MERCY ON US,
GOD WHO WRESTLES AND EMBRACES US.
SHATTER OUR ILLUSIONS,
REFUSE YOUR COMFORT OF ANGELS,
FEED OUR HOPE AND OUR HUNGER
WITH THE ADVENTUROUS FAITH
OF YOUR SPIRIT
UNTIL GRACE IS OUR ONLY SUFFICIENCY.
AMEN.

Reading

Luke 4:1-13

Prayers of concern

- for those who experience life as a wasteland

Chant

I WAITED, I WAITED ON THE LORD.
I WAITED, I WAITED ON THE LORD.
HE BENT DOWN LOW AND REMEMBERED ME
WHEN HE HEARD MY PRAYER.

- for those who are lost, or without meaning or value in their lives
- for stateless, dispossessed, or migrant peoples

Closing responses

Leader: The desert will sing and rejoice
ALL: AND THE WILDERNESS BLOSSOM WITH
FLOWERS.

Leader: All will see the Lord's splendor,
ALL: SEE THE LORD'S GREATNESS AND POWER.

Leader: Tell everyone who is anxious,
ALL: BE STRONG, AND DON'T BE AFRAID.

Leader: The blind will be able to see,
ALL: THE DEAF WILL BE ABLE TO HEAR.

Leader: The lame will leap and dance,
ALL: THOSE WHO CAN'T SPEAK WILL SHOUT.

Leader: This is the promise of God.
ALL: GOD'S PROMISE WILL BE FULFILLED.

7 PROMISED LAND

Call to worship

Leader: The Lord says: When the time comes,
I will answer the prayers of my people.

Left: I will betroth you to myself forever
Right: With integrity and justice, with tenderness and love.

Left: I will betroth you to myself with faithfulness,
Right: And you will come to know me.

Left: I will say: You are my people,
Right: And you will answer: You are our God.

Left: For once you were outside mercy.
Right: But now you have been given mercy.

ALL: THIS IS OUR HOPE, OUR LIVING HOPE.
WE SHALL BE GLAD.

Leader: The Lord says: When the time comes,
heaven and earth will answer each other
and I will love the unloved.

Readings

Joshua 4:1-7, 19-25; 5:10-12 ; Isaiah 58:6-12

Psalm or song

Sing to God with joy and gladness / Sent by the Lord / Blessed be God / O bless the Lord / Heaven and earth / Heaven is singing for joy / The God of heaven / No one will ever be the same

Symbols of the promised land

Suggestions for these might include milk and honey in the comb, bread and flowers, or fruits, all of which people may share with one another; or rooting plants, seeds that people might plant; musical (percussive) instruments with which to make a joyful noise; paints or clay with which to play.

Silence to reflect

On the varied meanings that "promised land" has for each one of us.

A time of witness or exchange about meanings of "promised land"

Chant

MAY THE WORDS OF OUR MOUTHS...

Blessing and repentance

Leader: God, our passionate life,
we bless you for the infinite beauty of created things—
sand, wind, wave, and the wings of the eagle—
for the love of land and people,
for the vine and the fruit and the good wine.
We bless you for the endurance of hope,
for the promise of renewal,
and for fleeting moments on the mountaintop.

ALL: BLESSED ARE YOU, GOD OUR PASSIONATE LIFE.

Leader: But if we have forgotten those who bear the marks
          of exile, desert, home, upon their hands and feet
          and suffer them to go on bleeding,
          if we have dismembered the body of God,
ALL: HAVE MERCY ON US, GOD WHO BRINGS US
          DOWN TO EARTH.
          GROUND US IN JUSTICE,
          ROOT US IN RIGHT RELATIONSHIP,
          GIVE FLESH TO OUR WORDS AND WORSHIP
          WITH THE BREATH AND PEACE OF YOUR SPIRIT
          UNTIL JOY IS OUR ONLY HOLY, COMMON
          GROUND.
          AMEN.

Readings
   Luke 24:13-35; John 15:16-17

Prayers of concern
- for all sick or grieving people
- for new or renewing communities and nations

Chant
   THROUGH OUR LIVES AND BY OUR PRAYERS
   YOUR KINGDOM COME.
   - for those caught up in war or violence
   - for those who are especially dear to us
   - for cooperative relationship with the earth and with
     one another

Closing responses
Leader: Look at your hands,
          See the touch and the tenderness
ALL: GOD'S OWN FOR THE WORLD.

Leader: Look at your feet,
          See the path and the direction
ALL: GOD'S OWN FOR THE WORLD.

Leader: Look at your heart,
          See the fire and the love
ALL: GOD'S OWN FOR THE WORLD.

Leader: Look at the cross,
          See God's Son and our Savior
ALL: GOD'S OWN FOR THE WORLD.

Leader: This is God's world.
ALL: WE WILL SERVE GOD IN IT.
          AMEN.[3]

Leaving song
Hallelujah we sing your praises / Jesus Christ is waiting / Amen Alleluia / For yours is the kingdom / Behold I make all things new

People may go out singing, since the journey goes on. Alternatively, the liturgy may end with a joyful acclamation, a **Gloria** *or* **Alleluia..**

8 *Local Church Pilgrimage*

Many churches have anniversaries, patronal festivals, and dedication services that can be enhanced by a time spent remembering places of particular importance in the church building and celebrating what such places evoke.

---

[3] Ibid.

In larger churches, it may be possible to physically move the congregation around the building in procession, singing an appropriate song or chant as they move from one venue to another. (Remember that people on the move cannot read words easily, so it is better to have a repetitive song that may range from a simple **Gloria** *to* **We are marching in the light of God.)** *In smaller churches, it may be sufficient either for the worship leader to move from one place to another or to have different leaders who stand at the various places of significance.*

What is said at each place may range from a reminder of its importance, to personal testimonies from different people at each location followed by shared corporate prayer.

This type of pilgrimage was originally used in a very large Anglican church in Leeds, where 120 people walked through the building and into the halls. It has also been used in small Methodist chapels.

The first thing is to identify places of significance. Here are some:

The door
Where some people enter and others pass by

The font
The place of common entry into the community of the church

The crossing
(Or altar steps, etc.) where people take vows of marriage

The pulpit
From which successive preachers have proclaimed the word of God

The table or altar
Where Christ is host and which links us with the church in heaven

The notice board
Which reminds us of the range of activities that happen in the church

The kitchen
Where people, often unthanked, prepare food (and that may be a place of cooking for a soup kitchen, etc.)

Here are examples of what might be said at two such places:

The door
This is the door through which we enter church on Sundays. It is also the door past which many walk, some of whom have been turned away from faith by the unwelcoming or judgmental nature of churches they once went to.
Let us pray for people who we dearly wish would find their way into the church, saying their first names aloud if any so wish.
(Names...silence...chant/song)

The altar/table
This is the communion table where Jesus Christ invites us to share in a meal where he is host. This is the table

around which generations of people have gathered. So here we may remember those who once sat with us at God's table on earth and who now sit at God's table in heaven, and in gratitude we name them.
(Names...silence...chant/song)

Even if the pilgrimage is going to move people around the building, it is good to have different people involved at each place of significance. To simplify matters, one person might lead the way and enable the prayer, while others say words, which they have devised, appropriate to the various locations.

Chant(s)

Door: *Here I stand at the door and knock;* **Font:** *Pour out, I will pour out;* **Crossing:** *Gloria;* **Pulpit:** *Deus de Deo;* **Table:** *Behold the Lamb of God;* **Notice board:** *Kumbaya;* **Kitchen:** *Let the giving of thanks*

HEALING

Since its beginning, the ministry of healing has played a vital and central part in the life of the Iona Community. We believe in the integrity of creation: "And God saw that it was very good." We believe that this integrity, broken by sin, has been restored in Jesus Christ; that we are called to recognize it and to realize it, to live undivided lives, and to work for the healing of divisions wherever we encounter them. The healing of broken bodies, of divided communities and nations, and of the earth itself and our relationship with it are all part of the integrity to which God calls us. They are all part of the ministry of healing.

Therefore, it is a ministry in which justice is as important as medicine; in which reverence for the earth (which may show up as recycling—or just cycling) is as important as respect for the person suffering from mental illness, in which the health of the body politic matters as much as the health of the body personal. Indeed, they are inextricably linked. George MacLeod used to say, "It is blasphemous to pray for

Margaret with bronchitis, if we are not prepared to do something about the damp housing which causes her bronchitis."

The ministry of healing is not only an exterior one. We are also invited to the healing of the divisions and splits in our own lives—the separation of the spiritual and the material is simply not possible if we believe that Jesus really lived in the flesh, was incarnate, and made holy/whole the human body. So we cannot separate our actions from their consequences, our freedom from our responsibility, our lives as individuals from our lives as persons in community. We are invited into the community of God.

This community, we believe, extends over the limitations of time and space. We are part of the communion of saints; our wholeness is inclusive, not exclusive. Even in death, we are not divided.

The three liturgies in this section include a liturgy of prayers for healing, including the laying on of hands; a liturgy for laying down and letting go of what has been in order to move into a greater wholeness; and a liturgy of thanksgiving for the communion of saints.

Notes on Prayers for Healing

A service of prayer for healing gives an opportunity to pray for individuals and communities who are in need and also for those present to share in and receive the ministry of the laying on of hands. The way the service is organized will need to be sensitive to the experience and tradition of both worshippers and worship leaders. The following are a few notes for guidance, both theological and practical.

1. The ministry of healing is not something to be practiced in secret or to be limited to particular individuals. It is the work of the whole Christian community,

and it is as much a part of the Christian life as prayer and service.

2. The New Testament evidence is that both Jesus and the Christian community prayed for the sick and laid hands on them when they prayed. We know in our daily lives that it is often touch, the hand on the shoulder, the hug of a friend, the cuddle of a child, that lets us know that we are loved. Touch, often more than words, is a way of giving physical expression to our prayers and concerns for each other.

3. Christian healing is about wholeness. Sickness is not limited to physical inability. Our past experience of hurt, our tangled emotions, and our inability to forgive or be forgiven, all make us less than whole and in need of healing.

4. The prayer for healing is about communities as well as individuals. Justice and healing walk hand in hand. The things that cause people to be hurt sometimes require a political solution arising out of our prayer. Our worship and our daily lives belong together.

5. To be involved in the healing ministry requires our willingness to be involved in the process of change. We may find ourselves called to listen, to visit, to support, to forgive. We may find ourselves involved in social and political action that will not only challenge the way things are, but that will challenge our attitudes and values as well.

6. The healing ministry is a shared ministry. The healer is God, who makes us whole and can use each one of us, broken as we are, to express God's healing and love. It is appropriate that people should, if they choose, both receive and take part in ministry, and it is appropriate to invite people to do so.

7. A short repeated prayer accompanying the laying on of hands enables the whole congregation to focus on what is happening.

8. If possible, the laying on of hands should take place in the midst of the congregation, so that everyone is as much involved as possible.

9. People and communities are prayed for by name because each person and situation is known to God, not as a problem to be solved, but as people who are accepted and understood and loved. We trust God to answer our prayers for healing, but we do not know how or when healing will happen. We trust God to act in love.

10. Praying for healing is in no sense a rejection of the work of medicine, which is also a gift of God. Prayer is not an alternative but a complement to other forms of healing, and a recognition that healing comes in many ways, and is in essence concerned with wholeness, not simply with cure.

9 | *Brokenness and Wholeness: A Service of Prayers for Healing*

Opening responses

Leader: We come in worship to God
ALL: IN OUR NEED, AND BRINGING WITH US
THE NEEDS OF THE WORLD.

Leader: We come to God, who comes to us in Jesus,
ALL: AND WHO KNOWS BY EXPERIENCE
WHAT HUMAN LIFE IS LIKE.

Leader: We come with our faith and with our doubts,
ALL: WE COME WITH OUR HOPES
AND WITH OUR FEARS.

Leader: We come as we are because it is God who invites
us to come,
ALL: AND GOD HAS PROMISED NEVER
TO TURN US AWAY.

Song

*Jesus Christ is waiting / We lay our broken world /
Out of our failure to create / Those who wait on the Lord*

Prayers of approach and confession

We are here, God.
We have felt your touch in the sunlight,
seen your power in the salt waves.
We have wondered at your mystery in the stars,
and we marvel that the maker of the universe
knows us by name.
We are here, God.
WE ARE HERE TO PRAISE AND WORSHIP YOU.

We are here, Jesus.
We know that you came to find us.
We have listened to your words
and smiled at your stories.
We have felt the warmth of your love,
and we thank you that you have called us friends.
We are here, Jesus.
WE ARE HERE TO PRAISE AND WORSHIP YOU.

We are here, Holy Spirit.
We are grateful for your presence,
grateful for the way you bring us close—
for the way you comfort us and challenge us
and keep us right.
We are here, Holy Spirit.
WE ARE HERE TO PRAISE AND WORSHIP YOU.

We are here, God,
in this moment, in this place.
And we thank you that you are here with us.

You know us, God.
We do not have to pretend with you.

In the silence of your love, we bring you
the things that trouble us,
that harm us,
that make us feel ashamed or afraid.

Silence

God have mercy on us.
CHRIST HAVE MERCY ON US.
God have mercy on us.

Silence

> Listen to the words of Jesus,
> words that we can trust:
> "Don't be afraid.
> Your sins are forgiven.
> I love you.
> Come and follow me."
> Thanks be to God.
> AMEN.

Readings

Song
We cannot measure how you heal / A touching place/
Lay your hands gently upon us / Take this moment /
When our Lord walked the earth

Prayers of intercession
Please feel free to name places and names in the silences.

> We are your people, God.
> In this time and place,
> you have called us to pray for those in need.

> We pray for the people whose names the world knows,
> whose stories are told daily in the news...

Silence

> God in your mercy
> HEAR OUR PRAYER.

> We pray for people in places of suffering,
> whose names only you and their friends
> and families know,
> and whose lives you cherish...

Silence

> God in your mercy
> HEAR OUR PRAYER.
>
> We pray for the people whose names and lives we know,
> those who today are in pain or distress or trouble, those
> who are happy, those who are sad ...

Silence

> God in your mercy
> HEAR OUR PRAYER.
>
> We pray for ourselves, God.
> You know each one of us by name.
> Make us into the people you want us to be,
> And when that hurts,
> Reassure us how much you love us.
> God, we bring you ourselves and our prayers
> In Jesus' name.
> AMEN.

Prayer for the Laying on of Hands

Those present who wish to receive the laying on of hands are invited to take a place at kneelers or chairs set out in a circle. Those who wish to share in this ministry should also come and stand behind those kneeling or sitting. In turn, hands are laid on the head or shoulders of those who kneel or sit. They may then move back to allow others to take a place.

It is quite appropriate both to receive and to share in the laying on of hands if so wished.

> SPIRIT OF THE LIVING GOD,
> PRESENT WITH US NOW,

ENTER YOU, BODY, MIND, AND SPIRIT,
AND HEAL YOU OF ALL THAT HARMS YOU,
IN JESUS' NAME, AMEN.

Closing prayer

Watch now, dear Lord,
with those who wake or watch or weep tonight,
and give your angels charge over those who sleep.
Tend your sick ones, O Lord Christ,
rest your weary ones,
bless your dying ones, soothe your suffering ones,
pity your afflicted ones, shield your joyous ones,
and all for your love's sake. *(St. Augustine)*
AMEN.

Closing responses

Leader: For loving the world and knowing our names,
thank you, God.

ALL: THANK YOU, GOD.

Leader: For your strength that fills us
and your love that heals us,
thank you, God.

ALL: THANK YOU, GOD.

Leader: For your presence here with us today
and for your hand that leads us into tomorrow,
thank you, God.

ALL: THANK YOU, GOD.

Leader: Come bless us, hold us, wrestle with us,
warm us in your embrace,

ALL: FOR WE ARE YOUR PEOPLE
AND YOU ARE OUR JUSTICE AND JOY.
AMEN.

If this liturgy is to be part of a service of Holy Communion, the service may continue after the closing prayer with the Preparation of the Gifts/Peace.

10   *A Liturgy for Laying-Down and Letting Go*

This liturgy is appropriate for sad times and situations of ending, leaving, or departing; perhaps for leaving a job or moving, even to a new country; perhaps for the ending of a relationship; perhaps for a member of a family or community moving on. Sensitive care should be taken about the location of the liturgy, which should have meaning and significance for the person or persons involved.

As Columba laid down his books
and the security of a monastery,
SO WE LAY DOWN WHAT IS PAST
AND LOOK TO THE FUTURE.

As Aidan and Cuthbert let go
and traveled hopefully on,
SO WE LET GO HURT AND PAIN
AND TRAVEL WITH HOPE.

As Hilda changed direction
and relinquished cherished plans,

SO WE LEAVE BEHIND FAMILIAR PATHS
AND TAKE NEW STEPS INTO THE UNKNOWN.

Song

Prayer of confession
Merciful God,
for the things we have done that we regret,
forgive us;
for the things we have failed to do that we regret,
forgive us;
for all the times we have acted without love,
forgive us;
for all the times we have reacted without thought,
forgive us;
for all the times we have withdrawn care,
forgive us;
for all the times we have failed to forgive,
forgive us.

For hurtful words said and helpful words unsaid,
for unfinished tasks
and unfulfilled hopes,
God of all time
forgive us
and help us
to lay down our burden of regret.

An act of contrition
*People may write what they wish to lay down on a piece of
paper, distributed beforehand, and place it at the foot of a
cross, in a boat (coracle), or in a rubbish bin. Where appropriate, these may be carried out, launched forth, or burnt.*

Alternatively, people could be invited to place a lit candle by a symbol of new beginnings (e.g., a sandal, keys, an A to Z, a book open on a fresh page).

It may be helpful to invite people to sow seeds of hope in a central pot, or sow individual ones, reminding them that we can't sow seeds with a closed hand.

Dandelion clock

Hope is a dark elusive child
curled in the womb
cradled in our arms.
It can be lost,
disappear,
blown on the wind like a dandelion clock.

Its going,
its ebbing away
leaves us
grieving,
empty,
hopeless.

But is a hopeful word.

But even as the gossamer
powder puff
disintegrates,
the seeds are carried
to cling to distant crevices.
As it recedes
it reseeds
to grow again.

God, giver of peace,
grow hope within and around us.
God of steadfast love,
never leave us hopeless.

A time of silence for reflection

Litany of letting go
I let go:
window and door
house and home
memory and fear.
I let go the hurt of the past
and look to the hope of the future.
I let go,
knowing that I will always carry
part of my past (part of you) with me
woven into the story of my life.

Help me/us, Christ my/our brother,
to softly fold inside
the grief and the sadness,
to pack away the pain
and to move on,
taking each day in your company,
traveling each step
in your love.

To finish
Pilgrim God,
our shoes are filled with stones,
our feet are blistered and bleeding,
our faces are stained with tears.

As we stumble and fall,
may we know your presence
in the bleeding and the tears
and in the healing and the laughter
of our pilgrimage.

11 | *A Liturgy for the Communion of Saints*

Ideally, worship should happen in a circle, with space in the center for people to move back and forward. A cross should be placed in the middle of the floor and around it should stand four candles.

Four objects are required to signify four stages of life. These might be:

birth and infancy	• a rattle
childhood	• a teddy bear
adolescence	• a CD, cassette, record, or yearbook
adulthood	• a set of keys

These should be in the possession of one person who will lay them out at the appropriate time. Everyone should also have, if possible, a pencil or pen. Everyone should be given an order of worship to which is stapled four triangles encompassing three circles. This is an ancient Celtic sign for a saint, sometimes found on the sleeves or hems of ancient garments.

The liturgy should be led by a number of people. There is no need for one voice or person to monopolize the parts. But it would be helpful if someone reviewed the order and rehearsed unknown songs before beginning worship. It is best if the worship takes place with dimmed lighting.

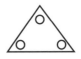

Opening reading

Reader: Bright, bright
The fellowship of saints in light,
Far, far beyond all earthly sight.
No plague can blight, no foe destroy.
United here they live in love:
O then above how deep their joy.

Set free
By Jesus' mortal wounds are we,
Blest with rich gifts—and more shall be.
Blessings has he in endless store:
Some drops are showered upon us here:
What when he hear the ocean's roar.[1]

or

Reader: Sniveling Zacchaeus, fiddler of books,
Hated by all but his fraternal crooks;
Blind Bartimaeus, unkeen to keep silence
Shouts from his bench in the beggars' alliance.

Thomas the cynic, the seeker of proof,
Doubts eyewitness stories and keeps quite aloof;
And shy Nicodemus, avoiding daylight,
Prefers anonymity granted by night.
A well-seasoned widow, alone at a well,
With four or five husbands, if only she'd tell;
A Roman centurion, proud of his power,
Confronts his own weakness in death's fatal hour.

---

[1]From *Threshold of Light,* edited by E. de Waal and A. M. Allchin, copyright 1986 by Darton, Longman, and Todd Ltd. Used by permission of the publishers.

And Martha and Mary, both numbed by their grief,
Unable to cope or find hope in belief;
And James and John, brothers, beloved by their
mum,
Obsessed by their seats in the kingdom to come;
And Peter with loyalty left in the lurch.
What a risk!—
"It is on this rock, I'll build my church."

Song

From Erin's shores Columba came / The strangest of saints

Prayer A

Leader: O High King of Heaven,
in the early days, when the church was young,
you called, in the wake of the apostles,
princes, and common folk to carry the gospel
to unbelieving lands.
Thus Patrick and Columba, Bride and Aidan
nurtured communities of faith
on these and other shores.

ALL: FOR THEM AND FOR ALL ANCIENT SAINTS
WHO BROUGHT CHRIST'S WORD TO CELTIC
LANDS
WE PRAISE YOU;
AND WE ASK THAT IN THESE LATER DAYS
THE ZEAL OF EARLY PIONEERS
MAY STILL INFUSE YOUR CHURCH.
AMEN.

or

Prayer B

Leader: Lord Jesus Christ,
you built your church on the rock of
redeemed humanity.
Through Peter and Paul
through Columba and Margaret
through Luther, Teresa, John XXIII, and Bonhoeffer
through all the saints of every age
you extended, reformed,
and diversified the household of faith.

ALL: WE, WHO INHERIT THEIR WORK TODAY
AND REAP FROM WHAT OTHERS HAVE SOWN,
BLESS YOU FOR ALL OUR MOTHERS AND
FATHERS
IN GOD.
LIKE THEM, MAY WE SO LOVE AND SERVE
YOUR KINGDOM
THAT GENERATIONS YET UNBORN
MAY BENEFIT FROM OUR WITNESS;
AND, WHEN THE GRACE OF LIFE ON EARTH
SHALL END,
FIND FOR US A PLACE
IN THE COMPANY OF HEAVEN,
FOR YOUR LOVE'S SAKE.
AMEN.

Words from the Saints

These or other short passages may be used, of which the first should be biblical:

Reader 1: A word from St. Paul:
Be always humble, gentle, and patient.
Show your love by being tolerant to one another.
Do your best to preserve the unity
which the Spirit gives you
by means of the peace which binds you together.
There is one body.
There is one Spirit.
There is one hope
to which God has called his saints.

Reader 2: A word from St. Teresa:
Be careful lest praise from others harms you,
especially when people tell you that you are
more saintly than others.
Remember how John the Baptist was extolled
then beheaded,
and how our Lord was praised on Palm Sunday
then derided on Good Friday.
Struggle with your own heart
against dangerous flattery.

Reader 3: A word from St. Francis:
Our place is to be with the suffering,
the lepers, the starving.
In the depths of their hearts,
as in the hearts of even the saintliest person,
there sleeps a horrible, unclean larva.
Lean over it and say to this larva, "I love you,"
and it will sprout wings and become like a butterfly.

O God of love, we bow to your power.
Come and kiss us, and accomplish your miracle.

Song
Ipharadisi

Meditation
Those whose lives touched ours

Four people should read this meditation, each section being preceded by the singing of the chant, during which the person who has the four symbols lays them, one at a time, beside a candle. During the meditation, participants might want to write the name of someone who comes to mind on one of the triangles of paper.

After all the sections have been read and all the symbols are out, the chant is sung repeatedly as people place their "saints" beside the appropriate symbols.

Chant
UBI CARITAS ET AMOR
UBI CARITAS, DEUS IBI EST.
("Where there is love and caring, God is there")
or
I AM THE VINE AND YOU THE BRANCHES
PRUNED AND PREPARED FOR ALL TO SEE,
READY TO BEAR THE FRUIT OF HEAVEN
IF YOU BELIEVE AND TRUST IN ME.
First symbol is placed

Voice 1:   Before I was born,
            you prayed for me;
            and when I moved from the womb to the world,
            your arms cradled me;
            and you sang funny songs,
            and you made sense of my gurgling language,
            and you held my hand till I slept,
            till I walked,
            till I lost my fear,
            till I was old enough to let your hand go.

Chant
Second symbol is placed
Voice 2:   When I was young,
            you prayed for me;
            when I broke my heart or bruised my skin,
            you cared for me;
            when I was keen to learn,
             you taught me;
            you watched my eyes bulge
            with the wonder of the world.
            You heard me repeat you;
            you let me cheat you;
            you often said yes and sometimes said no.
            And even today,
            I am enriched and restrained
            by what you did then.

Chant
Third symbol is placed
Voice 3:   When I left childhood,
            you prayed for me;
            when I was stubborn with my parents,

I could talk to you;
when I felt awkward with my body,
I felt comfortable with you.
And though you gave me good advice,
you saw me ignore it;
and though you gave me liberty,
you saw me abuse it;
and though you spoke of God,
you saw I did not want to know;
but still you held me through the difficult days
and I reap the benefit now.

Chant
Fourth symbol is placed

Voice 4:   Since I've become the adult
that I longed to be,
you've prayed for me;
when I had to cope with my failures,
you've accepted me;
when I was unsure of myself,
you've believed in me;
when I've stood on the brink of decisions,
you've stood beside me;
and when doubts had their day
and faith seemed remote
and the church irrelevant,
you've let God touch me.

Chant
*Sung repeatedly as triangles are placed near
appropriate symbols. Silence*

Closing song

O God, thou art the Father / For all the saints who've shown your love

Blessing

The leader begins and thereafter people may add names as appropriate after which all share the response. The leader concludes with final sentence.

Leader: The God of Abraham and Sarah
ALL: STAY WITH US NOW

Leader: The God of Moses and Elijah
ALL: STAY WITH US NOW

Leader: The God of Andrew, Peter, James, and John
ALL: STAY WITH US NOW

Leader: The God of Mary of Magdala
ALL: STAY WITH US NOW

Other names, biblical or otherwise, may be added here.

Leader: The God of our Lord and Savior Jesus Christ,
crucified, dead, risen, and ascended,
keep us in the commonwealth of heaven
now and evermore.
ALL: AMEN

ACTS OF WITNESS AND DISSENT

The Rule of the Iona Community commits its members to action for justice and peace in society. Our Justice and Peace Commitment, which is a point of departure rather than final destination, has as its sixth point the belief that "social and political action leading to justice for all people, and encouraged by prayer and discussion, is a vital work of the church at all levels," and as its eighth point the commitment to "engage in forms of political witness and action, prayerfully and thoughtfully, to promote just and peaceful social, political and economic structures." It is as a basic tenet of faith that members of the Iona Community engage in political activity, rather than as attachment to any particular political agenda.

But our engagement is constantly driving us into prayer. As George MacLeod, the founder of the Iona Community, wrote, "There are evenings when our prayer life is refreshing: but analyzed, they turn out to be the times when the pressures have been so weighty that you have simply had to go with them to God. But this is precisely the recovery of the knife-edge. The religious moment flowers from the practical." Nowhere is this more true than on the knife-edge of political and social engagement.

Many of the most significant acts of worship for members of the community on the mainland have not been in churches. They have been outdoors, on demonstrations and marches and picket-lines, outside military bases and the Ministry of Defence, in city squares and at embassies. Equally importantly, though perhaps less dramatically, they have been in homes and community centers, in schools and factories and hospitals—all the places where people struggle on a knife-edge and we among them. At the very least, we can take our bodies and our prayers and say with them, "I beg to differ." We can witness to our conviction that "it is better to light a candle than to curse the darkness."

Erik Cramb, a member of the community who is an industrial chaplain on Tayside, wrote about his involvement on the picket line in the Timex dispute in Dundee:

> We can stand on the sidelines and roundly condemn the attempts of Timex to force down wages in Dundee, and so we should. But we cannot pretend we're clean, we cannot pretend it's nothing to do with us. Those who seek to maximize our pension funds and our endowment policies are among the casino's biggest players...
>
> Greed, timidity, dishonesty, hopelessness, tears, exploitation, manipulation, violence, anger, betrayal, denial, decency, loyalty, unity, humor, forgiveness, generosity, solidarity—all the great themes of the faith were there for anyone who had eyes to see and ears to hear. The hope of new life beyond the current turmoil was never entirely lost—buds of faithfulness, of redemption ever present. To stand on the picket line was to be in the touching place, in the learning place, in the expectant place, to be where sin was, and was confronted by something better. Thank God, I was there!

12 | *Witness for Peace :*
Celebration of Life in Death

A peace liturgy adapted from a service held at Faslane Trident Submarine Base on 27 October 1986

Introduction

Voice 1:   I looked at the earth—it was a barren waste; at the sky—there was no light. I looked at the mountains—they were shaking, and the hills were rocking to and fro. I saw that there were no people; even the birds had flown away. The fertile land had become a desert and its cities were in ruins.

Voice 2:   Reading from *Deuteronomy 30:19*
This day I call heaven and earth as witnesses against you that I have set before you life and death, blessings and curses. Now choose life, so that you and your children may live.

Facing and naming the powers of death
A brief explanation is given of what goes on at this particular military establishment, and of its destructive power.
All stand in silence for two minutes facing the powers.

Song
By the waters of Babylon

Prayer of repentance
in which we acknowledge our own complicity in the forces of death

Leader: Forgive us, Creator God,
for we have seen into the abyss and not drawn back.
We pray for those of us who have the political power to make life or death decisions.

ALL: WE HAVE SEEN INTO THE ABYSS
AND NOT DRAWN BACK.
SUNG: KYRIE ELEISON

Leader: We pray for those of us who can see no choice but to work in the industries of death.
ALL: WE HAVE SEEN INTO THE ABYSS
AND NOT DRAWN BACK.
KYRIE ELEISON

Leader: We pray for those of us who pay our taxes or make our profits out of the industries of death.
ALL: WE HAVE SEEN INTO THE ABYSS
AND NOT DRAWN BACK.
KYRIE ELEISON

Leader: We pray for those of us who have failed to speak loudly enough or take action boldly enough to challenge the industries of death.
ALL: WE HAVE SEEN INTO THE ABYSS
AND NOT DRAWN BACK.
KYRIE ELEISON

Leader: We pray for those of us who have been too confused or helpless to know what to do.
ALL: WE HAVE SEEN INTO THE ABYSS
AND NOT DRAWN BACK.
KYRIE ELEISON

Leader: We know that with you life is abundant, and that you can make all things new.
ALL: WE REJOICE IN YOUR HOPE.

Reading
Romans 8:35–39
Leader: Who shall separate us from the love of Christ?
ALL: LET US CELEBRATE HOPE IN THE VIBRANT LIFE OF CHRIST.

Song
Those who wait on the Lord

Commitment to life
Leader: In the midst of hunger and war
ALL: WE CELEBRATE THE PROMISE
OF PLENTY AND PEACE.

Leader: In the midst of oppression and tyranny
ALL: WE CELEBRATE THE PROMISE
OF SERVICE AND FREEDOM.

Leader: In the midst of doubt and despair
ALL: WE CELEBRATE THE PROMISE
OF FAITH AND HOPE.

Leader: In the midst of fear and betrayal
ALL: WE CELEBRATE THE PROMISE
OF JOY AND LOYALTY.

Leader: In the midst of hatred and death
ALL: WE CELEBRATE THE PROMISE
OF LOVE AND LIFE.

Leader: In the midst of sin and decay
ALL: WE CELEBRATE THE PROMISE
           OF SALVATION AND RENEWAL.

Leader: In the midst of death on every side
ALL: WE CELEBRATE THE PROMISE
           OF THE LIVING CHRIST.[1]

Words of encouragement

Reader: To do and dare—not what you would, but what is right. Never to hesitate over what is in your power, but boldly to grasp what lies before you. Not in the flight of fancy, but only in the deed there is freedom. Away with timidity and reluctance! Out into the storm of event, sustained only by the commandment of God and your faith, and freedom will receive your spirit with exultation.

Dietrich Bonhoeffer [2]

or

Prayer for strength (spoken)

Leader: Lord, we do not pray for easy lives,
           we pray to be stronger people.
           We do not pray for tasks equal to our powers,
           but for powers equal to our tasks.
ALL: WE STAND TOGETHER FOR LIFE
           IN THE MIDST OF DEATH.

---

[1]Attributed to Edmund Jones. Reproduced by permission of Stainer & Bell.

[2]Dietrich Bonhoeffer, *Letters & Papers from Prison,* HarperCollins Publishers.

Song

Be not afraid / God give us power / Sent by the Lord / Oh Lord, hold my hand

Act of witness

During the singing, those who wish to make a particular witness for peace come forward. Actions can range from lighting a candle for those who have inspired us, to symbolic burning of missiles, to acts of civil disobedience.

Blessing

Leader: Go forth into the world in peace; be of good courage; hold fast that which is good; render to no one evil for evil; strengthen the fainthearted; support the weak; help the afflicted; honor all people; love and serve the Lord, rejoicing in the power of the Holy Spirit.

ALL: AMEN.[3]

or

Leader: Sisters and brothers arise.
            Arise and lift your hearts, arise and lift your eyes, arise and lift your voices.
            The living God, the living, moving Spirit of God sends us out together in witness,
            in celebration,
            in struggle;

---

[3]From *The Prayer Book as Proposed in 1928*, © The Central Board of Finance of the Church of England; reproduced with permission.

reach out toward each other;
our God reaches out toward us.[4]

13 *Peace Liturgy for a Wet Day*

Since most demonstrations seem to take place in the pouring rain, this is a shortened version, in which no one needs bits of paper that would otherwise get soggy.

Leader: *Reading from Deuteronomy 3:19 and John 10:10 An explanation is given about the base or military installation.*

Song
Kyrie Eleison
Two-minute silence
Leader: We come to celebrate life.

Symbol of hope
(Not a candle!) Plant a flower, name people who have inspired us, weave a rainbow with colored threads, hand in a petition, etc.

Prayer
Hold hands and pray together: the Lord's Prayer or the Prayer for Peace, or have people share a story or sign of hope or keep silent. After each one, all say:
THE HOPE OF THE WORLD

---

[4]Elizabeth Rice, *No Longer Strangers: A Resource for Women and Worship,* edited by Iben Gjerding and Katherine Kinnamon © 1983 WCC Publications, World Council of Churches, Geneva, Switzerland.

Song
Amen siakudumisa / Allelujah / We shall overcome /
We are marching in the light of God

Blessing

Leader: Let us share the good news of peace in the world:
            The peace of Christ be with you.
ALL: AND ALSO WITH YOU.

14 *Cursing the "Money Boys":*
An Act of Witness for
Economic Justice

The service begins with the congregation divided in two, facing each other. RHS and LHS indicate either side of the church or room. The leader of worship stands in the middle.

Leader: Jesus said: Blessed are the comfortable, for God
            has shown them his favor.
RHS: OH NO HE DIDN'T!
LHS: OH YES HE DID!

Leader: Jesus said: Blessed are those who have good pen-
            sion funds, for God has shown them his favor.
RHS: OH NO HE DIDN'T!
LHS: OH YES HE DID!

Leader: Jesus said: The strong and powerful will inherit
            the earth.
RHS: OH NO HE DIDN'T!
LHS: OH YES HE DID!

Leader:	Jesus said: Blessed are the winners, for they will inherit everything.
RHS:	OH NO HE DIDN'T!
LHS:	OH YES HE DID!

Leader:	Jesus said: Don't do anything to undermine the existing order—to do so is to go against God.
RHS:	OH NO HE DIDN'T!
LHS:	OH YES HE DID!

Leader:	Jesus said: Look after yourself; then if you have something left over, give a coin to the poor.
RHS:	OH NO HE DIDN'T!
LHS:	OH YES HE DID!

Leader:	Jesus said: God is a nice old man, who doesn't want anyone to rock the boat.
RHS:	OH NO HE DIDN'T!
LHS:	OH YES HE DID!

Reading

Matthew 21:12-17

A member of the congregation narrates the story of the entry of Jesus into Jerusalem, which is enacted. Jesus strides down between the two groups and overturns the tables with a bang, scattering the money. The leader allows the uneasiness and the silence to grow.

| Leader: | Jesus said: Blessed are the poor in spirit, for the kingdom of God is theirs. |
| ALL: | KILL HIM! |

Leader: Jesus said: How hard it is for those who have riches to enter the kingdom of heaven!

ALL: KILL HIM!

Leader: Jesus said: It is easier for a camel to go through the eye of a needle than it is for a rich man to enter the kingdom of heaven.

ALL: KILL HIM!

Leader: Jesus said: Blessed are the meek, for they shall inherit the earth.

ALL: KILL HIM!

Leader: Jesus said: Blessed are the peacemakers: they shall be called the children of God.

ALL: KILL HIM!

Leader: Jesus said: Blessed are you when you suffer insults and persecutions and calumnies of every kind for my sake.

ALL: KILL HIM!

Leader: Jesus said: Do not be anxious about tomorrow: tomorrow will look after itself.

ALL: KILL HIM!

Leader: Jesus said: Alas for you who are rich: you have had your time of happiness!

ALL: KILL HIM!

Leader: Jesus said: Sell your possessions and give to the poor.

ALL: KILL HIM!

Leader: Jesus said: Where your treasure is, there your heart will be also.

ALL: KILL HIM!

Leader: Jesus said: Alas for you when all speak well of you!

ALL: KILL HIM!

Leader: Jesus said: If you want to be my disciple, you must take up your cross and follow me.

ALL: KILL HIM! KILL HIM! KILL HIM!

Silence

Reading of recent newspaper reports from different parts of the church about the disparity between rich and poor, about Third World debt, about the role of world bankers. Then these words of George MacLeod are introduced:

Reader: Fifty years ago, George MacLeod, founder of the Iona Community, wrote these words:

Something must be done about the money boys who run our world. It is urgent that the whole issue of international monetary finance be reviewed.

Have you ever queried the bankers? I have. Try the lower echelon of bankers, and most of them will say, "These things are too high for us, we cannot attain unto them," but a small minority will whisper, "You've got something there, boy; isn't it extraordinarily cold weather for so late in the month of May?"

Try the upper echelon of bankers. I have. I

wrote to the top man of a London bank, a charming man, asking his comments on a similar document to the Haslemere Declaration *[Declaration about world poverty].* He replied that the figures were inaccurate. I immediately asked which figures, but had no reply.

They are in training for the job of international bankers. They know what is good for us. Don't consult us, the paltry crowd. But do they know what is good for us? Or are they sowing the seeds of the next war?[1]

Song
For the healing of the nations (or another)

Readings
Psalm 24; Ephesians 6:10-20

Short meditation on the word
It should emphasize not only the global interlocking of the "principalities and powers" that keep poor people in debt, but also individual attitudes toward money.

Prayers of intercession

Song
Almighty Father of all things that be (or another)

Closing responses
Leader: We will not offer to the Lord
ALL: OFFERINGS THAT COST US NOTHING.

---

[1]Quoted in Ron Ferguson, *George MacLeod,* HarperCollins Publishers, 1990, p. 364.

Leader: Go in peace, to love and serve the Lord.
ALL: WE WILL SEEK PEACE AND PURSUE IT.

Leader: Glory be to the Father and to the Son
           and to the Holy Spirit.
ALL: AS IT WAS IN THE BEGINNING, IS NOW AND
           EVER SHALL BE,
           WORLD WITHOUT END.
           AMEN.

15 | *Common Ground: An Act of Witness Against Racism*

This act of witness should take place with people seated in a circle or semicircle so that they can face each other with a space in the midst of them. It may be appropriate to hold it in a place that represents neutral ground for people of differing backgrounds and faiths, for example, a school or community center.

Voice 1:   *Listen to the words of a British Asian woman:*
            We are told that human rights law is about unit-
            ing families. But Asian people see regularly that
            Britain's immigration laws are separating fami-
            lies. After three years of waiting, I am completely
            sickened and worn out by the delay and the
            worry. As British citizens, we have no right to
            family life. Yet women in Europe may enter
            Britain with husbands, children, and entire family
            without application, without interviews. There
            will be no racial justice for us until the law is
            changed. The politicians have failed us. People of
            faith must give a lead.

*From a statement made by a Muslim woman in Manchester
Cathedral on Human Rights Day 1989, before an audience of
Muslims, Sikhs, Hindus, Jews, and Christians.*

Leader: A welcome to you all.
            Some of us have strong faith. In some of us, faith
            falters.
            But we are all here as children of God,
            as inhabitants of one earth.
            We bring to this place our fears and anxieties,
            our visions and dreams for the future.
            We bring our politics and our prayers,
            our strengths and our weaknesses,
            our issues and our concerns;
            and we lay them out on the ground,
            hoping that the middle ground may become
            not waste ground,
            not battleground,
            but common ground.

*People may, at this point, bring out symbols or placards rep-
resenting some of their concerns, e.g., a passport, No Entry
signs, and lay them in the space or on a table in the middle.*

Song of hope and solidarity
*He came down / Let's walk together / Come now, O Prince of
Peace / If you believe and I believe*

Voice 2:   Listen to these words from the World Council of
            Churches:
            Every human being, created in the image of God,
            is a person for whom Christ has died. Racism,

which is the use of a person's racial origins to determine the person's value, is an assault on Christ's value and a rejection of his sacrifice.[1]

Voice 3:   Listen to these words from Matthew 23:23:
[Jesus said:] How terrible for you, teachers of the Law and Pharisees! You hypocrites! You give to God one-tenth even of the seasoning herbs such as mint, dill and cumin, but you neglect to obey the really important teachings of the Law, such as justice and mercy and honesty. (TEV)

Prayers for forgiveness

Leader: Helder Camara said that
it is very difficult to create awareness
in the privileged.

LET US PRAY:
God, you call us to see and hear and understand,
to open our eyes and ears and hearts,
to be aware.
Forgive us for our false pride and complacency,
for our unthinking consumerism.

ALL: LORD HAVE MERCY UPON US.

Leader: Forgive us for our insularity,
for our reluctance to accept new ways.

ALL: LORD HAVE MERCY UPON US.

---

[1]*World Council of Churches' Statement and Actions on Racism 1948-1979,* © 1980, WCC Publications, World Council of Churches, Geneva, Switzerland.

Leader: Forgive us for our complaining,
for growing bitter and sorry for ourselves,
for becoming hardened and indifferent
to the pain of others.

ALL: LORD HAVE MERCY UPON US.

Voice 1: "Why do you treat Asian people like this? Don't
you understand that Jesus was an Asian? Would
you do this to Jesus?"
*(A Muslim woman, angry at the treatment of
Asian families under UK immigration laws)*

Silence

Leader: God, make us aware, make us repentant.
We turn to you.
Heal us of our privileged blindness,
and make us whole.

ALL: AMEN.

Sharing stories

*People now have the opportunity to share their stories in
whatever form they wish to tell them, and to be heard without interruption or dismissal.*

Sharing memories

*People are now invited to share in a "collective memory-
making" in which reflections on a particular theme or issue
(e.g., law, family, travel) are either written on a large sheet of
paper or written on small pieces and collected in a basket. By
"remembering" different aspects of the same thing, a collective
memory is created that is presented for prayer and may be
printed and used later.*

During this time a song or chant may be sung.

Song or chant
Send out your light / Word of the Father / Listen, Lord / Come, Holy Spirit

Readings
Isaiah 58:6-12 or passages from the Koran and the Talmud may be used, as well as the scriptures of other faiths

Prayers of concern
During the prayers of concern a candle may be lit after each petition and placed in the center space beside the symbols or placards of concern and the collective memory.

Leader: Come, God,
               listen to the calling of those with nowhere to turn.
               At the point where support fails,
               the majority turns away,
               and we/they are alone.

ALL: WE CANNOT REMAIN SILENT
               BECAUSE WE FEAR THE AUTHORITIES
               AND DO NOT WANT TO ROCK THE BOAT.[2]

Leader: We remember those who suffer
               as a result of family breakup
               or unjust immigration or nationality laws.

ALL: WE CANNOT REMAIN SILENT
               BECAUSE WE FEAR THE AUTHORITIES
               AND DO NOT WANT TO ROCK THE BOAT.

---

[2]*The Road to Damascus,* CIIR/Christian Aid.

Leader: We remember those who suffer harassment or
          abuse in the street or school or workplace
          as a result of their religion or skin color.

ALL: WE CANNOT REMAIN SILENT
          BECAUSE WE FEAR THE AUTHORITIES
          AND DO NOT WANT TO ROCK THE BOAT.

Leader: God of justice, give us voice, take away our fear,
          shake up our prejudices, and move us to a differ-
          ent place, to stand on common ground with those
          who struggle for justice.

ALL: AMEN

Common ground statement
*Before the reading of this statement on racism, people may
be invited to leave their places and stand in the center space
as a sign of solidarity with its intention.*

Leader: RACISM IS A SIN AGAINST GOD
          AND AGAINST FELLOW HUMAN BEINGS.
          IT IS CONTRARY TO THE JUSTICE
          AND THE LOVE OF GOD.
          IT DESTROYS THE HUMAN DIGNITY
          OF BOTH THE RACIST AND THE VICTIM.
          WHEN PRACTICED, IT DENIES ANY FAITH
          OR CONVICTION WE PROFESS TO HOLD.
          WE CONDEMN RACISM IN ALL ITS FORMS.

Reading
Luke 4:18-19

ALL: THE SPIRIT OF THE LORD IS UPON ME,
          BECAUSE HE HAS CHOSEN ME
          TO BRING GOOD NEWS TO THE POOR,

HE HAS SENT ME
TO PROCLAIM LIBERTY TO THE CAPTIVES
AND RECOVERY OF SIGHT TO THE BLIND,
TO SET FREE THE OPPRESSED,
AND ANNOUNCE THAT THE TIME HAS COME
WHEN THE LORD WILL SAVE HIS PEOPLE.
(TEV)

Song
Stand firm

Closing prayer

Leader: God, lead us that we may stand firm in faith for justice.

ALL: TEACH US LOVE. TEACH US COMPASSION. ABOVE ALL, OUT OF LOVE AND COMPASSION, TEACH US TO ACT.
AMEN.

A SANCTUARY AND A LIGHT

The Prayer for the Iona Community (see below in *An Act of Prayer*) asks, "if it be your holy will, grant that a place of your abiding be continued still to be a sanctuary and a light." This is usually assumed to be a reference to the community's residential centers on Iona and Mull, and yet the prayer is one for the community, not the buildings. There is a sense in which the prayer can also be for the embodiment of these characteristics in the people.

Sanctuary and *light* are, of course, first and foremost attributes of God, who is "our refuge and our strength," the Lord who is "our light and our salvation." God is the one in whom we find the secure love, the safe place that all of us long for and need in order to be truly free; and yet God leads us on and out into the world, into challenge and adventure and discipleship.

The movement of coming home and going out is a constant dynamic of faith; the two exist in a creative relationship in which each needs the other. Without the light that leads us out, our security becomes complacent and self-absorbed. But without the sanctuary, the safe place of return (whether in our communities, our homes, or in our solitude with God), our activity becomes brittle, exhausted, and often fearful.

The three liturgies here are all about right relationship of sanctuary and light. The first focuses on the experience of women, for whom it has often been a distorted relationship; the second is especially for children and adults to share, for a right relationship of sanctuary and light is a crucial part of life and faith nurture; and the third is an act of prayer for members of the community when they gather.

16 *Women: Refuge and Adventure*

This liturgy was written for use in a Scottish context (The-new, also known as Enoch and mentioned later in this liturgy, was the mother of St. Mungo or Kentigern, patron saint of Glasgow), but it can be adapted for use in other contexts with the insertion of other names—a fruitful and interesting area of research into the hidden history of women in the church.

Leader: Let us enter into the presence of God.
               God, Creator Spirit,
               You are Breath.
ALL: BREATHE NEW LIFE INTO US.

Leader: You are Fire.
ALL: INFLAME OUR COLDNESS WITH LOVE.

Leader: You are Wind.
ALL: LET US RIDE ON YOUR WHIRLING WINGS.

Leader: You are Refuge.
ALL: OUR SHELTER IS IN YOU.

Song
The love burning deep (or another)

Leader: Come and share the story of women. Let us listen to their voices, honor their lives, affirm their gifts, weep for their suffering, and celebrate their embodiment in the image of God.
ALL: FOR THEIR VOICES ARE OUR VOICES,
               THEIR BODIES ARE OUR BODIES,
               THEIR STRUGGLES ARE OUR STRUGGLES,
               AND WE SHARE A COMMON HUMANITY.

Litany of violence

Voice 1: I am Hagar, slave woman banished to wander in the desert.

Voice 2: I am Tamar, raped by my brother and then reviled.

Voice 3: I am Jepthah's daughter—killed as an offering to God.

Voice 4: I am all the nameless, voiceless, forgotten ones.

Leader: Women of the Bible, violated and abandoned, where shall you find refuge?

ALL: OUT OF THE DEPTHS WE CRY TO YOU, GOD. HEAR OUR CRY AND LISTEN TO OUR PRAYER.

Voice 1: I am Thenew, a Christian convert, chased from my home for refusing my father's choice of husband, raped in a field, stoned and abused, twice sentenced to death, homeless when my child was born.

Leader: Mother of Mungo, hidden from history, where shall you find refuge?

ALL: OUT OF THE DEPTHS WE CRY TO YOU, GOD. HEAR OUR CRY AND LISTEN TO OUR PRAYER.

Voice 2: I am four thousand Scottish women, persecuted, tortured, and accused of witchcraft; stripped, strangled, and burned in a frenzy of terror.

Leader: Women punished for being different, where shall you find refuge?

ALL: OUT OF THE DEPTHS WE CRY TO YOU, GOD. HEAR OUR CRY AND LISTEN TO OUR PRAYER.

Voice 3:   I am numberless women all over the world,
            this day and every day, beaten and bloodied,
            battered and bruised by the men they live with.
Leader: Women, your home is where the hurt is,
            where shall you find refuge?
ALL: OUT OF THE DEPTHS WE CRY TO YOU, GOD.
            HEAR OUR CRY AND LISTEN TO OUR PRAYER

Silence, for reflection on these and others, known and unknown, who have been victims and survivors of violence.

Leader: For too long we have worshipped a god of fear and
            anger,
            a god of injustice and exclusion,
            a god who values men more highly than women,
            a god who abandons us in our pain and sorrow.
            Let us repent of all the harm done to women
            in the name of that mean and dangerous god
            and banish him from our hearts, our homes, our
            communities.
SUNG: KYRIE ELEISON

Leader: Spirit of love, under your strong and tender wings
            there is refuge for all who are exploited, harassed,
            patronized, demeaned, and abused. Shield, nur-
            ture, and restore us to wholeness and integrity in
            our personal and corporate lives. In your shelter,
            let us create a safe place to be ourselves, to explore
            new possibilities, to share friendship, and to sus-
            tain each other in the struggle for liberation.
            AMEN.

Psalm 27
This can be read either responsively or by one voice, or it can be sung.

Reading
    Luke 8:42b–48

Litany of empowerment
During this litany candles are lit for each group of women honored. In a small gathering each person might read in turn. The sections should be adapted and added to as appropriate for those present, and space should be given to invite participants to speak names or share their own stories of women.

Leader: God, the refuge you offer is no hiding place from the world. It is a sanctuary for survivors, where you warm us with shared experience and kindle in us a passion to struggle against cruelty, exclusion, and oppression. Your wings lift us high with hope and laughter. Soaring above loneliness and pain, we see a vision of what might be. So let us celebrate the adventure of women who act with courage and perception to lighten our way.

Voice 1:   This is the light of Ruth, a foreigner who journeyed into the unknown for the sake of love and loyalty to Naomi, and who acted with initiative to change their lives for the better.

ALL: FOR THIS WE PRAISE YOU
AND CLAIM RUTH'S POWER OF SOLIDARITY.

Voice 2: This is the light of Joanna and Susanna, who knew and loved Jesus, who comforted, challenged, and inspired his ministry, who witnessed a new way of living.

ALL: FOR THIS WE PRAISE YOU,
AND CLAIM THE DISCIPLES' POWER
OF COMMITMENT.

Voice 3: This is the light of Thenew, who was resolute in faith and prevailed against the worst men could do to find a safe home for herself and her child.

ALL: FOR THIS WE PRAISE YOU
AND CLAIM THENEW'S POWER
TO OVERCOME ADVERSITY.

Voice 4: This is the light of Celtic women who integrated action and contemplation, passion for creation, with respect for learning.

ALL: FOR THIS WE PRAISE YOU
AND CLAIM THE CELTIC POWER
OF ROOTED WISDOM.

Voice 5: This is the light of women caregivers, nurses, midwives, and doctors, present with compassion, expertise, and humor throughout the cycle of life and death.

ALL: FOR THIS WE PRAISE YOU
AND CLAIM THE HEALERS' POWER
OF TOUCH.

Voice 6: This is the light of women who have struggled to build bridges of hope, justice, and reconciliation in a world of poverty, suspicion, and war;

as peacemakers, politicians, community cam-
paigners, and good neighbors.

ALL: FOR THIS WE PRAISE YOU
AND CLAIM THE ACTIVISTS' POWER
TO DREAM DREAMS.

Voice 7: This is the light of women who have shattered the
silence of violence by speaking out in the face of
indifference and by offering places of safety in
which fear is banished and self-esteem affirmed.

ALL: FOR THIS WE PRAISE YOU
AND CLAIM THE COLLECTIVE POWER
OF RIGHTEOUS ANGER.

Voice 8: This is the light of untold women's lives, shining
through hardship, sustained in hope, cherished in
tenderness, poured out in passion, glowing with
glorious life-giving love. It is the light of our
mothers and grandmothers, our sisters and
daughters, our friends and partners and lovers. It
is the light of refuge and adventure.

All join hands for blessing.

ALL: FOR THIS WE PRAISE YOU
AND BLESS EACH OTHER
AND CLAIM THE POWER OF WOMEN
TO LIVE IN FREEDOM, JUSTICE,
AND WHOLENESS.
HALLELUJAH! *(either as a song or as a shout of
acclamation)*

17 | *A Safe Place and a Light: A Liturgy for Children and Adults*

Opening responses

Leader: When we are happy,
When we are full of fun and laughter,

ALL: GOD WELCOMES US.

Leader: When we are angry,
When people let us down and make us sad,

ALL: GOD WELCOMES US.

Leader: When we are tired,
When we need to stop and curl up and rest,

ALL: GOD WELCOMES US.

Leader: God of welcome,
God whose door is always open,

ALL: WE ARE GLAD TO MEET YOU HERE.

Song

Heaven is singing for joy / Halle, halle, halle / Come host of heaven's high dwelling place / Amen siakudumisa

The Word of God

Leader: Listen to God's Word. First we hear some words from the book of Zechariah that tell us about the sort of place God wants our world to be. *Then we'll listen to a child's retelling of the story of Zacchaeus.*

Reader 1: God gave this message to Zechariah:
I have longed to help Jerusalem
because of my deep love for her people.

I will return to Jerusalem and live there.
It will be known as the faithful city.
Once again old men and women
so old that they use a stick when they walk
will be sitting in the city squares.
The streets will be full again
of boys and girls playing...
People will sow their crops in peace,
the vines will bear grapes,
the earth will produce food,
and there will be plenty of rain...

These are the things you must do:
speak the truth to one another,
in the courts give real justice,
the kind that brings peace.
Do not plan ways to hurt each other;
do not tell lies about each other.
Have courage;
do not be afraid.
Love truth and love peace.

Reader 2: One day there was a man called Zacchaeus. He was working with his pen and paper. Zacchaeus said to the people, "Pay twelve coins." He gave the Romans ten coins and he kept two coins for himself and put them in his pocket. So he was rich. He had a beautiful house.

One day Jesus came and Zacchaeus wanted to see him, but he had one problem—he was little, so he could not see over the people's heads. He saw a tree and climbed up it. Jesus saw him and said, "What are you doing up there?" Everyone was laughing. Jesus said, "Get down here Zacchaeus," so he got down. Jesus said, "I am coming up to your house for tea." Zacchaeus was nervous–he got all his servants to tidy up–they got out all the best knives and forks and spoons and it all looked beautiful.

Jesus and Zacchaeus sat at the table and were talking. They drank all the wine and ate the food. Zacchaeus said, "I am sorry about all of the things I have taken from the poor people. I will give them their money back." Jesus said, "That's what I want to hear–you have got everything– sort it out." Then they finished their tea.

Praying for ourselves

Voice 1:   Let us pray:
God, we live in a world that needs to change.
We are part of the world.
We do things that hurt each other,
things that are wrong.
There are things that we need to sort out.

Silence to think about these things.

ALL: GOD, WE ARE SORRY.
WE WANT TO DO THINGS DIFFERENTLY.

Voice 2:   Let us listen to God's words,
words for those who want to change.
In Jesus, God says to us:
"I know you are sorry.
I forgive you.
I love you.
Don't be afraid."

ALL: GOD, THANK YOU.
            THANK YOU FOR YOUR LOVE.
            AMEN.

Song
Take this moment, sign, and space / He came down

Sharing our stories

Leader: For all of us it is important to know that we are
            loved, that people care for us and stand up for us.
            We need food to eat and safe places to sleep and
            work and play. For all of us, it is good to have
            places where we feel comfortable and safe, people
            we enjoy being with, and friends and family who
            love us. In a minute, can you get into groups of
            four or five people, maybe with people you don't
            know very well, and talk together about the
            places where you feel safe and the people you
            enjoy being with, and, if you've time, try and
            work out what makes those places feel safe and
            good. When you hear some music, it will be time
            to be quiet and come back to your seat. So go and
            talk together about the places and people that
            make you feel safe and good.

*People get up and go to share their stories. Worship leaders
may invite groups to share their findings with the congregation.*

Praying for others

Leader: We are going to pray now for people around the
            world, who, like us, need to know that God loves
            them. We light candles as we pray, as a sign that

God brings light and love into the world. After we
have lit the first five larger candles, and when the
music plays, you are invited to come and light a
candle for anyone you know, or have heard about,
who needs to know that God loves them.

Voice 1:   We pray for the people of Africa...

Add words for specific situation.
Someone brings a candle from the midst of the congregation
and places it centrally, possibly on a map of the world.

Voice 2:   We pray for the people of the Americas...
(as Voice 1)

Voice 3:   We pray for the people of Asia...

Voice 4:   We pray for the people of the Pacific...

Voice 5:   We pray for the people of Europe...

Some music is played or a chant sung as people come and
light candles and place them centrally in trays of sand.

Leader: Into the dark places of our world
            Where people are frightened and hungry,
ALL: GOD, BRING LIGHT, BRING LOVE.

Leader: Into places where people are fighting,
            Into places where people have no homes,
ALL: GOD, BRING LIGHT, BRING LOVE.

Leader: Into the places where we feel unsafe,
            Into situations that hurt us and scare us,
ALL: GOD, BRING LIGHT, BRING LOVE.

Leader: We ask our prayers in Jesus' name
            and in the Holy Spirit's power.
ALL: AMEN.

Song
No one will ever be the same

Closing responses
*Read alternately by each half of the congregation, e.g.,
children/adults, left side/right side.*

A: God, keep us safe in danger,
B: Give us courage and keep us loving.

A: God, help us to speak the truth,
B: To stand by those who need our help.

A: God, give us friends who love us,
B: Places and people that help us grow.

A: God, send us on our way rejoicing
B: And welcome us safely home.

ALL: AMEN.

18 *An Act of Prayer*

For use when members of the community gather and suitable for use in house groups, meetings, etc.

Silence

The Community responses

Leader:	The world belongs to God,
ALL:	THE EARTH AND ALL ITS PEOPLE.
Leader:	How good and how lovely it is
ALL:	TO LIVE TOGETHER IN UNITY.
Leader:	Love and faithfulness meet,
ALL:	JUSTICE AND PEACE EMBRACE.
Leader:	If the Lord's disciples keep silent,
ALL:	THESE STONES WOULD SHOUT ALOUD.
Leader:	Open our lips, O God,
ALL:	AND OUR MOUTHS SHALL PROCLAIM YOUR PRAISE.

Song and/or psalm

Prayer

Leader:	Holy God, Maker of all,
ALL:	HAVE MERCY ON US
Leader:	Jesus Christ, Servant of the poor,
ALL:	HAVE MERCY ON US.
Leader:	Holy Spirit, Breath of life,
ALL:	HAVE MERCY ON US.

Silence

Leader: I confess to God, and in the presence of all God's people, that I have sinned in thought, word, and deed, and I pray God to have mercy on me.

ALL: MAY GOD HAVE MERCY ON YOU, PARDON AND DELIVER YOU FROM YOUR SINS, AND GIVE YOU TIME TO AMEND YOUR LIFE.

Leader: Amen.

ALL: WE CONFESS TO GOD, AND IN THE PRESENCE OF ALL GOD'S PEOPLE,
THAT WE HAVE SINNED IN THOUGHT, WORD, AND DEED,
AND WE PRAY GOD ALMIGHTY
TO HAVE MERCY ON US.

Leader: May God have mercy on you, pardon and deliver you from your sins, and give you time to amend your life.

ALL: AMEN.

Leader: Turn again, O God, and give us life

ALL: THAT YOUR PEOPLE MAY REJOICE IN YOU.

Leader: Make me a clean heart, O God,

ALL: AND RENEW A RIGHT SPIRIT WITHIN ME.

Leader: Give us again the joy of your help,

ALL: WITH YOUR SPIRIT OF FREEDOM SUSTAIN US.
AMEN.

Scripture reading
Followed by discussion, exposition, or silence

Prayer for the Iona Community

Leader: O God, who gave to your servant Columba the gifts of courage, faith, and cheerfulness and sent people forth from Iona to carry the word of your gospel to every creature, grant, we pray, a like spirit to your church, even at this present time. Further in all things the purpose of our community, that hidden things may be revealed to us and new ways found to touch the hearts of all. May we preserve with each other sincere charity and peace, and, if it be your holy will, grant that a place of your abiding be continued still to be a sanctuary and a light, through Jesus Christ our Lord.
AMEN.

Prayer for our own reshaping

ALL: O CHRIST, THE MASTER CARPENTER,
WHO AT THE LAST, THROUGH
WOOD AND NAILS,
PURCHASED OUR WHOLE SALVATION,
WIELD WELL YOUR TOOLS IN THE WORKSHOP
OF YOUR WORLD,
SO THAT WE WHO COME ROUGH-HEWN TO
YOUR BENCH
MAY HERE BE FASHIONED
TO A TRUER BEAUTY OF YOUR HAND.
WE ASK IT FOR YOUR OWN
NAME'S SAKE.
AMEN.

Prayers for the members of the Iona Community

As listed for the day in Miles Christi

Leader: May they not fail you
ALL: NOR WE FAIL THEM.

Prayers of thanksgiving

The Lord's Prayer

Leader: Lord, teach us to pray.
ALL: OUR FATHER IN HEAVEN
           HALLOWED BE YOUR NAME.
           YOUR KINGDOM COME, YOUR WILL BE DONE
           ON EARTH AS IN HEAVEN.
           GIVE US TODAY OUR DAILY BREAD.
           FORGIVE US OUR SINS
           AS WE FORGIVE THOSE WHO SIN AGAINST US.
           SAVE US FROM THE TIME OF TRIAL
           AND DELIVER US FROM EVIL.
           FOR THE KINGDOM, THE POWER, AND THE
           GLORY ARE YOURS
           NOW AND FOREVER.
           AMEN.

Silence

Closing responses

Leader: In work and worship
ALL: GOD IS WITH US.

Leader: Gathered and scattered
ALL: GOD IS WITH US.

Leader: Now and always
ALL: GOD IS WITH US.
AMEN.

RESOURCES

BEGINNINGS AND ENDINGS OF WORSHIP

1 *Come Among Us, Jesus*

Come among us, Jesus,
You whom the angels worship
and children welcome.
COME, JESUS, AND MEET US HERE.

Come among us, Jesus,
You who hurled the stars into space
and shaped the spider's weaving.
COME, JESUS, AND MEET US HERE.

Come among us, Jesus,
You who walked the long road to Bethlehem
and lit a flame that dances forever.
COME, JESUS, AND MEET US HERE.

2 | *Lord, Your Constant Love Reaches the Heavens*

Lord, your constant love reaches the heavens
Your faithfulness extends to the skies
YOUR RIGHTEOUSNESS IS TOWERING LIKE THE
MOUNTAINS
YOUR JUSTICE IS LIKE THE DEPTHS OF THE SEA
We find protection under the shadow of your wings
We feast on the abundant food you provide
YOU ARE THE SOURCE OF ALL LIFE
AND BECAUSE OF YOUR LIGHT, WE SEE THE
LIGHT
Psalms 36:5-9 (TEV)

3 | *God of the Past*

God of the past, who has fathered and mothered
us,
WE ARE HERE TO THANK YOU.

God of the future, who is always ahead of us,
WE ARE HERE TO TRUST YOU.

God of the present, here in the midst of us,
WE ARE HERE TO PRAISE YOU.

God of life beyond us, within us,
WE REJOICE IN YOUR GLORIOUS LOVE.

4 | *Come, God*

Come, God.
Come walk with your people,

for you alone are our strength and glory,
AND WE PUT OUR TRUST IN YOU.

Come, God.
Come walk behind us, beside us, before us,
for you alone are our shelter and direction,
AND WE PUT OUR TRUST IN YOU.

Come, God.
Come, seek and find and put us right,
for you alone are the light in our darkness,
AND WE PUT OUR TRUST IN YOU.

Come, God.
We know you are near.
The sound of your footsteps sets us dancing.
HELP US TO PRAISE AND WORSHIP YOU.

5 | *For Christmas*

Opening Responses
God of creation, shaper of seas and stars,
of planets and of people,
GOD IS HERE WITH US.

God, born in Bethlehem,
gurgling, crying, laid in a manger,
GOD IS HERE WITH US.

God, breath of the universe,
flickering, dancing in the candle flame,
GOD IS HERE WITH US.

God, Immanuel, amongst us, within us,
WE BRING OURSELVES AND OUR DREAMS,
FOR WE WANT TO BE HERE WITH YOU.

Closing Responses

Mysterious God, confounding our expectations,
meeting us where we least expect to find you,
STAY WITH US NOW.

Child of the manger, healing our pain,
sharing our weakness,
STAY WITH US NOW.

Source of life,
birth of God within our own experience,
STAY WITH US NOW.

Stay with us in our frailty,
stay with us on our journey,
WALK BESIDE US, LIVE WITHIN US,
LEAD US TO GLORY, LEAD US HOME.

6 | Opening Responses for a Liturgy for Healing

If you come
in certainty or in confusion,
in anger or in anguish,
THIS TIME IS FOR US.

If you come
in silent suffering or hidden sorrow,
in pain or promise,
THIS TIME IS FOR US.

If you come
for your own or another's need,
for a private wound or the wound of the world,
THIS TIME IS FOR US.

If you come
and do not know why,
to be here is enough.
THIS TIME IS FOR US ALL.

Come now, Christ of the forgiving warmth,
Come now, Christ of the yearning tears,
Come now, Christ of the transforming touch,
THIS TIME IS FOR YOU.

7 *Name Unnamed*

Name Unnamed, whose intriguing presence
is closer to home than we dare imagine,
fill us with wonder of you
THAT WE MAY BE FILLED WITH WONDER OF
OURSELVES.

Name Unnamed, whose creativity is a river running,
startle us with diversity

and surprise us with difference
THAT WE MAY BE FILLED WITH WONDER OF
OTHERS.

Name Unnamed, whose mystery and concern is
revealed in Jesus,
reshape our perceptions,
reshape our patterns of living,
reshape our politics and prayer,
THAT WE MAY BE FILLED WITH WONDER OF A
WORLD MADE WHOLE.

8   *Invocation*

From the corners of the world,
from the confusion of life,
from the loneliness of our hearts,
GATHER US, O GOD.

To feed our minds,
to fire our imagination,
to free our hearts,
GATHER US, O GOD.

9   *Opening Preparation for Silent Service*

When the world tells us
we are what we do with
our activity, acumen, or achievement,
let us learn

WE ARE WHAT WE DO WITH OUR SILENCE.
When the world tells us
we are what we do with
our spending power, selling power, or our power of
speech, let us learn
WE ARE WHAT WE DO WITH OUR SILENCE.

When the world tells us
to drown the silent sufferings of others with indifference or noise,
or to forget the art of stillness even in the storm,
let us learn
WE ARE WHAT WE DO WITH OUR SILENCE.

When the world tells us
to rush in where angels fear to tread,
let us learn that angels listen first
before they take a step
for the voice of God in the silence...

Silence

SHORT PRAYERS

10 **Stories**

Lord Jesus, you told great stories.
They helped people make sense of their lives,
they revealed God in ordinary things,
they encouraged and changed people.

Make us more ready to share our stories.
Give us words where we are tongue-tied,
confidence to know our stories matter,
tact to know the right place to tell them.
Also, most importantly, make us ready to listen.

11 *Light*

Shining God,
even the darkness is not dark to you.
Shine in our darkness, light of our lives.

When we walk in the gray gloom of confusion,
when pain drains all the color out of life,
when we are paralyzed by the darkness of fear,
shine in our darkness.

When we know that others are walking in the darkness, give us courage to be light for them.

12 *After Psalm 131*

God, you love us with a tender love
like Mary, holding her child gently in her arms,
like Joseph, breaking with harsh tradition
to stand by his beloved and her baby.

Still our restless hearts to rest in you,
knowing ourselves loved.

13 | *Waiting*

God, so much of faith is waiting,
like a pregnant woman waiting in hope,
like a people under siege, holding out till relief comes,
like the soul lost in the darkness,
unable to see even a glimmer of light
yet stumbling through the night because somewhere
out ahead, day will surely break.
God, be with us in our waiting.

14 | *God of Light and Warmth*

O God, star kindler,
kindle a flame of love within us
to light our path in days of darkness.

O God, sun warmer,
warm us with your love
to melt the frozen hand of guilt.

O God, moon burnisher,
burnish the shield of faith
that we may seek justice
and follow the ways of peace.

15 | *Advent Antiphons*

These prayers take their pattern and inspiration from the
antiphons that traditionally have been part of the church's

liturgy during the last week of Advent. They recall people's experience of what God is like, and they call on God to come to our aid.

O God, you speak through your prophets
your words hold us and challenge us and keep us
right:
come and tell us the truths that we need to know
and write them into our hearts and lives.

O Lover of the little ones,
their Guardian and Defender:
come with your angels and cradle your children
and guide their stumbling feet
along the homeward roads.

O Maker of laughter,
who plays with Leviathan in the deep waters:
come stretch out your hands
to cuddle and tickle your children
through the moments of their days.

O Loving Mother, whose presence offends many
and delights many more:
come and help us to see clearly
the one in whose likeness we are made.

O Pilgrim God, abandoning that which is no longer
needed:
come with us on our journey,
show us how to travel lightly
keeping only what we need to grow.

O God, you love us
come, come quickly,
We need your help.

O Wind of God, you blow through
the holes in our defenses
and lay bare our fear:
come, breathe on us gently,
as at the beginning,
and give us life.[1]

16 *Creator God*

Creator God,
because you make all that draws forth our praise
and the forms in which to express it,
we praise you.
Because you make artists of us all,
awakening courage to look again at what is taken
for granted,
grace to share these insights with others,
vision to reveal the future already in being,
we praise you.
Because you form your Word among us,
and in your great work embrace all human experience,
even death itself, inspiring our resurrection song,
we praise you.
Yours is the glory.

---

[1]*A Book of a Thousand Prayers,* edited by A. Ashwin, HarperCollins
Publishers, 1996.

17 *Invocation for Lent*

Into a dark world
a snowdrop comes,
a blessing
of hope and peace,
carrying within it
a green heart,
symbol of God's renewing love.
Come to inhabit our darkness,
Lord Christ,
for dark and light
are alike to you.

May nature's white candles of hope
remind us of your birth
and lighten our journey
through Lent and beyond.

18 *Invocation for Mothering Sunday (Mother's Day)*

Come, Mother God,
come as an enfolding
nurturing presence,
come as steadfast love
to hold us.

Come, Mother God,
come as an enabling
strengthening force,

come as tough love
to let us go.

Come, Mother God,
come as friend and comforter
healing our wounds,
walking our way,
come as wounded healer
to make us whole.

PRAYERS FOR FORGIVENESS

19 *God of the Spirit of Kindness*

God of the spirit of kindness,
in the glory of earth and sea and stars,
in the kaleidoscope of color and shade and
shapeliness,
in the patterns of humor and tenderness and touch,
we celebrate your generosity.

Forgive us when we forget the gift in our every
breath,
the care that sustains our every moment,
the grace that can transform our every day.

Set us free from the prison of grudging hearts,
mean desires,
resentful spirits.
Give us the courage to act with justice
and generosity,
and draw us into love that does not calculate
or keep scores.

20 *Beloved God*

Beloved God,
we fear your judgment:
teach us to know it as our friend.
Your word has pierced us to the bone;
we are exposed, laid open to your sight.

Therefore, let us bless you,
for you come to us when we are most ashamed;
and when we long to hide our face from you,

you will not suffer us to turn away.
You call us by our name;
you touch us, raise us,
invite us into shameless love.
God our lover, know us, judge us,
turn us, wound us, demand of us,
forgive us.
We are yours.
We abandon ourselves to your love.
We trust you.

21 *Cross-carrying Jesus*

Cross-carrying Jesus,
As you stagger on your lonely journey
time slips
worlds reel.
Forgive us that we turn away
embarrassed
uncaring
despairing.
Help us to stay with you through the
dark night
to watch and to wait
to know the depths of your anguish
and to realize that you carry us,
forgive (even) us,
love us.
Forgive us
that we get on with our work unthinking
that we gamble, unknowing, with precious things.
Cross-carrying Jesus,

nailed to the tree of life,
forgive us
and grant us your salvation.

22 *This Day*

Voice 1: Cross-carrying Jesus,
woodcarved to foul purpose
tree of life
deep rooted in Golgotha's soil
arms stretched to embrace the world
cross
empty
Christ let loose in the world.

Voice 2: This day you will be with me in Paradise.

Voice 3: Who, me Lord?
Not me.
Not there.
I'm a thief.
I've stolen ladies' handbags,
Young girls' virginity.
I've diddled the books
and sold arms to Africa.

Voice 2: This day you will be with me in Paradise.
Beyond death in new life you will walk with me
down our street
round the corner, with the chip papers
blowing in the wind and into the
betting shop.

You will dine at the Ritz
lie in the gutters of Calcutta
and step into outer space with confidence.

Voice 3: Where, Lord?
Up there
or down here?
You confuse me.

Voice 2: Come with me through the gates
and we shall see.

23 *Lord of the Morning*

Bless to us, O God, this day, fresh made.
In the chorus of birds, bless us.
In the scent of blossom, bless us.
In the wet grass and the spring flowers, bless us.
Bless us and heal us,
for we come to you in love and in trust.
We come to you in expectant hope.

Silence

O God, give us a well of tears
to wash away the hurts of our lives.
O God, give us a well of tears
to cleanse the wounds,
to bathe the battered face
of our world.
O God, give us a well of tears
or we are left, like arid earth,
unsanctified.

Silence

Heal us and your grieving world
of all that harms us.
By the power of your resurrection
restore us to new life,
set us on new paths,
bring us from darkness to light,
help us to choose hope.

Jesus says, "Pick up your bed and walk."
Pick up the bed of your sorrows and fears,
pick up the bed of your grief and your sin,
pick up your life and come, come follow him.

24 *On the Side of Justice*

O God, you are on the side of justice,
and you call your people to be on that side too.
Where people are turned off food-growing land
so a few can make big profits,
where children work in factories for pennies,
where women ruin their health to feed their families,
not in the world of the past but the world of today.
LORD HAVE MERCY UPON US,
CHRIST HAVE MERCY UPON US.
God, forgive us if we profit from the suffering of
others,
remind us that we have power in our choices
if we act together.
Lead us to choose justice
in our politics, in our economics, in our churches.
Justice, beginning where we are.

25 *Rag and Bone Confession*

There are lumps under our carpet
that the vacuum won't vanguish.
There are cats tied in bags
would be off like a flash.
Skeletons in the cupboards
tap tap on the doors.
There is nothing hidden
but that's going to get out,
so let's get it over with, God.

Silence

There's a pile at the foot of the cross
of the things we could do without.
Make us glad we brought them to you,
who carries away the sins of the world,
and grant in their place
pardon and grace
and your call to be following always.

26 *Confession*

Together in worship, we face what we might not
face alone
  • that we are greedy, but refuse to love our bodies
  • that we are selfish, but refuse to love ourselves
  • that we are lazy, but refuse to work for peace
  • that we are human, but refuse to love the earth.
These we share in silence as we remember
our own faults and failings...

Silence

God of the turning tide,
change us so that the energy of your forgiveness

flows into bold and joyful action,
into a humility that is not defeatism,
into the strength and confidence to be vulnerable.

27 | ***Your Kingdom Come***

Lord,
you know that we love you,
and we know what you ask us to do—
but for those times when we have been too busy,
when we have been hard-hearted,
when we have been lukewarm,
we say, sorry,
and ask, for your forgiving love.
Prepare us for your way, O Lord.
YOUR KINGDOM COME, YOUR WILL BE DONE.

Lord,
you know our good intentions,
and we know your will—
but hold us back long enough to listen to those in
need
and to learn from them
and to learn of our own need.
Where we think we are sent, make us ready to
receive,
where we are keen to teach, make us ready to learn.
Prepare us for your way, O Lord.
YOUR KINGDOM COME, YOUR WILL BE DONE.

Lord,
you know our deepest desires,
and we know the vision of your kingdom—

we bring before you those elements in our lives
in need of your transforming power:
that which we misuse or neglect,
that which we most reluctantly let go of,
that which we believe is not good enough.
Inspire us and disturb us to examine our deepest
desires.
Prepare us for your way, O Lord.
YOUR KINGDOM COME, YOUR WILL BE DONE.

Lord,
you know our potential,
but what is your purpose for our lives?
In our uncertainty
and in the knowledge of your faithfulness,
prepare us for your way, O Lord.
YOUR KINGDOM COME, YOUR WILL BE DONE.

28 *Creator God*

Creator God,
by your design we are whole people,
yet we have sought to prise Word from flesh
to drain truth from life.
We have lived in our limits
touching the bounds for reassurance.
We have distrusted the vision
and sought to destroy the visionary.
KYRIE ELEISON/LORD HAVE MERCY
said or sung

Forgive us
when we have been willing to be entertained
but not changed,
when we have allowed our insights
to harden into clichés,
when we have spoken
only to consolidate our own position,
when we have called on you
only to hear the sound of our own voices,
when our celebrations have left others
with nothing to enjoy.
KYRIE ELEISON/LORD HAVE MERCY

Searching and creative Spirit of God,
who makes community
from the raw materials of our lives,
teach us the humility to learn from those
who know a true rejoicing
through Jesus Christ,
who simply revealed your glory.

WORDS OF FAITH

29 *Adoration*

We cannot tell
how much the sound of silence,
creation's beauty, gloriously aflame;
we cannot tell
how much the sight of starlit heavens
moves us to prayer,
to praise creation's Maker,
and our own.

We cannot tell
how much the son of Mary,
the man of Nazareth,
the son of God upon a tree;
we cannot tell
how much the man of sorrows
moves us to prayer,
to praise the One
who gives our lives
a meaning and a goal.

We cannot tell
how much the Spirit's comfort,
how much the wind of freedom
means to us.
We cannot tell—
for words cannot contain
the love beyond all loves,
the truth
that in the end
there is
only
God.

30 *After Psalm 19*

The sky does it simply, naturally
day by day by day.
The sun does it joyfully,
like someone in love,
like a runner on the starting-line.
The sky, the sun,
they just can't help themselves.
No loud voices, no grand speeches,
but everyone sees, and is happy with them.

Make us like that, Lord,
so that our faith is not in our words but in our lives,
not in what we say but in who we are,
passing on your love like an infectious laugh:
not worried, not threatening, just shining
like the sun, like a starry night,
like a lamp on a stand,
light for life—
your light for our lives.

31 *Birth*

To wait
to endure
to be vulnerable
to accept
to be of good courage
to go on
day after day after day;
to be heavy with hope
to carry the weight of the future

to anticipate with joy
to withdraw with fear
until the pain overcomes,
the waters break,
and the light of the world
is crowned.
Then the travail is over,
joy has overcome.

Lord of heaven and earth,
crowned with blood
at your birth,
delivered with pain,
bring new hope to birth
in your waiting world.
Bring fresh joy
to those who weep.
Be present
in all our dyings and birthings.

32 *Lifted High*

A little kid ran across the street,
runny-nosed, a bit scruffy,
tripping over almost.
She ran toward a man whose
arms were opened wide to
welcome her.
"Give us a swing, Jesus," she said,
and she felt herself lifted high,
and she saw the street and the sky whirling
around her, ablaze with color,

like a mixed-up rainbow.
She was laughing then—
excited, free,
gasping for breath.
"Enough," she said,
and she felt herself slowing down,
relaxing, safe, as Jesus
held her in his arms
and smiled...

Unless we become like little children,
Unless we risk that joy and abandonment,
Unless we run and ask and let ourselves
be lifted high,
We are never going to enter the kingdom of God.

33 *Lent Darkness*

Dragons lurk in desert spaces,
penetrating the mind with evil claw.
Serpent's teeth seek out the chinks
insidiously, relentlessly, gnawing on the bone;
searching out the interstices of muscle and sinew.

Such is the pain of the wilderness.
Alone, alone, alone,
Christ sits
in the waste place of abandoned pleas and
questions
until exhausted.
Finally
at last

the realization
comes
that in the end
there is only
God.

In the nighttime of our fears,
in the present reality of abandonment,
when family and friends
turn and run,
be present, ever-present God.
Be present with those
camped out in the fields of hopelessness
with refugees and homeless,
those who live lives of quiet desperation.
Be present until the desert places
blossom like the rose
and hope is born again.

34 | *Coming Home*

Written for someone joining the church
When you cross the borders of the desert
and head for home,
you do not want to turn back.
What you are heading for is a place of belonging,
a place where you can lay your body down.
Everything inside you is running—
you have run away often—
but this time you are running for home.

You will still be yourself,
still be restless sometimes and afraid,

but what beckons you now are bonds of loving
and, when all is said and done,
(and sometimes there is too much saying and too
little doing)
living where your life belongs is coming home.
Welcome to the family.

|35| *For My Mother*

"Underneath are the everlasting arms"—
loved words and loving—
reminding us of a God
who is always there,
like a mother with a young child,
knowing our needs,
catching us when we fall,
comforting, bearing, cradling, dancing, and
caressing.

Underneath are the everlasting arms:
words of encouragement
in moments of desolation
and loneliness;
words passed down from mother to daughter,
not in cold print but warm with faith.

Underneath are the everlasting arms:
now you are dying—
is it hard to let go?
For so long you have been there
to catch, to carry, and to care.
Listen, love, I want you to know

that I can cope:
first your faith nurtured me,
and your strength,
but now I have found my own.
Let go.
Into God's hands I commend your spirit:
Underneath are the everlasting arms.

36 *Circuit*

Based on a prayer from the Carmina Gadelica
I make my circuit
in the fellowship of my God
on the machair, in the meadow,
on the cold heathery hill,
on the corner in the open,
on the chill windy dock,

to the noise of drills blasting,
to the sound of children asking.

I make my circuit
in the fellowship of my God
in city street
or on spring-turfed hill,
in shop-floor room
or at office desk.

God has no favorite places.
There are no special things.
All are God's and all is sacred.
I tread each day

in light or dark
in the fellowship of my God.

Be the sacred Three of glory
interwoven with our lives
until the Man who walks it with us
leads us home
through death to life.

THANKSGIVING

37 *Thanksgiving for Community*

Thank you for our time in community,
for deep, if fleeting, friendships,
for those conversations late at night,
for the vulnerable intensity lubricated by laughter,
for the freedom to serve others
and to affirm ourselves
in the face of all that you know and we know of
our lives.
And we thank you for any signs that the churches
with which so many are disaffected
can yet be your body on earth in the community of
creation.

38 *Thanksgiving Prayer*

Thanks be to you, God, awesomely distant.
Thanks for the searing of shooting stars,
the colors of the planets in the night sky,
the space and power beyond our perceiving
that sparkles the sky of our lives with your caring.

Thanks be to you, God, uncomfortably close,
giving life to dead dry things
—the dance of pure stillness,
the beat of our hearts,
is your doing.

Thanks be to you, God, known in a body
who blessed as he lived,
who raised up our life

to be gathered as one, reaching out for the
kingdom.

39 *Hope Growing*

Hope growing,
silently, secretly,
like a child in the womb, fluttering;
putting out soft fingers,
hope, stretching, stirring.

Hope growing,
silently, secretly,
daring to breathe again
as footsteps recede
and danger retreats,
hope, stretching, stirring.

Hope growing
silently, secretly
swelling, burgeoning, bursting
until the flower opens,
the child is crowned,
the prisoner is released,
and hope is born.

God of all hopefulness,
for seeds of silent growth
and secret expectation,
we thank you.
Bring hope to birth in us;

release us that we may worship
in freedom and joy.

40 *All Shall Be Well*

For the greening of trees
and the gentling of friends,
we thank you, God.

For the brightness of field
and the warmth of the sun,
we thank you, God.

For work to be done
and laughter to share
we thank you, God.

We thank you, and know
that through struggle and pain,
in the slippery path of new birth,
hope will be born
and all shall be well.

41 *Thanksgiving*

Gracious God,
for your love for us
gentle as a shower
healing our pain
binding our wounds
WE GIVE YOU THANKS.

For your love for us
sure as the dawn

transforming our darkness
revealing your truth
WE GIVE YOU THANKS.

For your love for us
mercifully steadfast
calling us to you
raising us up
WE GIVE YOU THANKS.

For your love for us
encouraging questions
open to doubts
making us vulnerable
WE GIVE YOU THANKS.

Urge us on, O Christ,
to find wholeness
through serving you
by serving others
in the power of your Spirit.

42   *Midwife of Our Lives*

God of power and presence,
you are the midwife of our lives,
always drawing us on to be born again,
encouraging, exhorting, calming,
containing even death.
You pull us, kicking, into life,
breathe spirit into us.
We thank you for the gift in our breath,

the love that we make,
the hope that we cherish,
the grace that encompasses our darkest day.
In smallness and splendor, in storm and serenity,
we celebrate your care and creativity.
We rest in you, as trustingly as any baby.

43 *Jesus Our Faithful Friend*

Jesus our faithful friend,
we thank you for the precious gift of friendship,
for the people who accept us as we are,
love us even in our least attractive moments,
help us laugh at ourselves and laugh at life,
encourage us, support us, believe in us, value us.
Help us never to take friendship for granted,
but to tend it as a beautiful plant.

44 *Lord Jesus, It's Good to Know*

Lord Jesus, it's good to know
that you lived in the flesh,
walked where we walk, felt what we feel,
got tired, had sore and dirty feet,
needed to eat, and to think about
where the next meal was coming from.
But it's even better to know
that you enjoyed your food,
the feel of perfume on your skin,
the wind on your face, a child in your arms,
and the good wine at the wedding.

You didn't mind when people touched you,
even those who were thought of as unclean.
You kissed people with diseases
and laid your head on your friend's shoulder.
Thank you for understanding our bodily pains and
pleasures
and for valuing them.

45 *Great Thanksgiving*

*When this prayer is used, the words of institution are said in
the invitation to the Lord's table or in relation to the breaking
of the bread.*

Holy God, we praise you.
Let the heavens be joyful
and the earth be glad.

We bless you for creating the whole world,
for your promises to your people Israel,
and for Jesus Christ, in whom your fullness dwells.

Born of Mary, he shares our life.
Eating with sinners, he welcomes us.
Guiding his children, he leads us.
Visiting the sick, he heals us.
Dying on the cross, he saves us.
Risen from the dead, he gives new life.
Living with you, he prays for us.

With thanksgiving we take this bread and this cup
and proclaim the death and resurrection of our
Lord.

Receive our sacrifice of praise.
Pour out your Holy Spirit upon us
that this meal may be
a communion in the body and blood of our Lord.
Make us one with Christ
and with all who share this feast.
Unite us in faith,
encourage us with hope,
inspire us to love,
that we may serve as your faithful disciples
until we feast at your table in glory.

We praise you, eternal God,
through Christ your Word made flesh,
in the holy and life-giving Spirit,
now and forever. Amen.[1]

[1]From *The Book of Common Worship*, © 1993, Westminster/John Knox Press, p. 152.

CONCERN

46 *Praying for More*

God, Creator,
more than mother, more than father,
in love you spoke,
and there was the world
for which we now pray.

We pray for more than our speech can contain:
for trees and mountains,
fish and birds,
the species that come and go over time.

We pray for more people than we can ever meet,
and because we pray,
you can ask us to share your peace
with the victims of war.

And because we pray,
you can ask us why farmers are paid
not to grow crops
while sisters and brothers go hungry.
And because we pray,
you can ask us why our creative gifts are used
to destroy families and nations
and the world around us.

You can ask us,
because you know from experience
what our life is like,
so our prayer is a two-way talk.

And we pray,
in our world,
get your word in edgeways.

47 *New Ways*

God of our lives,
you are always calling us
to follow you into the future,
inviting us to new ventures, new challenges,
new ways to care,
new ways to touch the hearts of all.
When we are fearful of the unknown, give us
courage.
When we worry that we are not up to the task,
remind us that you would not call us
if you did not believe in us.

When we get tired
or feel disappointed with the way things are going,
remind us that you can bring change and hope
out of the most difficult situations.

48 *Moving House*

"When the last moving man left,
table and chairs were still
out in the yard.
We had so many belongings—
far more than we needed."

Holy Spirit,
for whom there is room in every home,

help to clear a way
through the clutter of possessions,
to make room for those who live there
to be fully themselves,
and for outsiders to be welcomed.

Spirit of hospitality, bless all
who share meals at our table—
even if it's still
out in the yard.

49 *Neighbors*

God with us,
you did not put us in the world alone;
you gave us people to live beside,
to keep us company,
to share skills and resources,
to stop us from getting bored.
Thank you for good neighbors—
people who are kind, people who are funny,
people who notice if something is wrong,
people we trust enough to leave our keys with.

God beside us,
sometimes we don't like our neighbors.
We can't believe you really meant them
when you said, "love your neighbors,"
did you God?
Not the nosey or noisy ones,
not the messy ones,
not the ones whose children don't behave,
whose dress or manners we don't like?

If you really do mean them, God,
We're going to need your help.
Help us not to be too quick to judge,
help us to hold out a hand of friendship,
help us to remember that loving our neighbors
is not what we feel, but what we do.

50 *The Shadow of the Dove*

When dawn's ribbon of glory around the world
returns
and the earth emerges from sleep—

May the shadow of the dove be seen
as she flies across moor and city.
Over the warm breast of the earth she skims,
her shadow falling on the watcher in the tower,
the refugee in the ditch,
the weary soldier at the gate.

May the shadow of peace
fall across the all-night sitting of a council
across the tense negotiators around a table.

May the shadow of hope
be cast across the bars of a hostage cell,
filling with momentary light
rooms tense with conflict,
bringing a brief respite,
a slither of gold across the dark.

May she fly untiring across flooded fields,
across a city divided by hate and fear,
across a town wreathed in smoke.

May the shadow of reconciliation,
the dove of peace with healing in her wings,
be felt and seen and turned toward
as she makes righteousness shine like the dawn,
the justice of her cause like the noonday sun.

Holy Spirit of love,
BRING HEALING, BRING PEACE.

51 *Thomas*

Put your hand,
Thomas,
on the crawling head
of a child
imprisoned
in a cot
in Romania.
Place your finger,
Thomas,
on the list of those
who have disappeared
in Chile.

Stroke the cheek,
Thomas,
of the little girl
sold in prostitution
in Thailand.

Touch, Thomas,
the gaping wounds
of my world.
Feel, Thomas,
the primal wound
of my people.
Reach out your hands,
Thomas,
and place them at the side of the poor.
Grasp my hands, Thomas,
and believe.

52   *Prayer Rosary*

Hiroshima,
Bosnia,
Belfast,
the names slip through our fingers
like bloodstained beads.

As we tell the story,
tell us,
tell us,
tell us,
the way
to peace.

Beirut,
Nagasaki,
Nuremberg,
still they come, countless numbers:
people hounded, refugees tramping the road
out of hell, into hell.

Where will it stop?
Show us,
show us,
show us,
the way to peace.

Five for sorrow,
ten for joy.
May what has been sown in pain
be reaped in hope.

53 ## *Prayer for Hiroshima Day: August 6th*

God, today in sorrow we remember, and we share our grief.

The few seconds of annihilating time
at Hiroshima and Nagasaki that seared itself
forever
into the depth of our present existence.
Those who died, those who wish they had died,
and those who live, never to forget:
WE REMEMBER.

The many thousands all over the world
who sighed with relief at the ending
of six long years of war.
Those who died,
those whose suffering made them long for death,
those whose experiences seared their lives
and hopes forever,

those who waited, mourned,
and lived lives of regret at home:
WE REMEMBER.

The scientists, politicians, engineers, technicians,
and members of the armed forces
who came to realize the awesome power and
responsibility of new technology,
and who live with the results of that knowledge:
WE REMEMBER.

The present generation,
growing up in a changed world,
overshadowed by the threat of extinction,
feeling helpless in the web of events:
WE REMEMBER.

We acknowledge our share of the pain and the
responsibility.
God, in Christ you showed us
that you are not removed from us
but share in our agony and suffering.
You are the mother holding her child from the
blast,
you are the tortured prisoner longing for release,
you are the war-weary soldier,
you are the scientist pacing the midnight hour,
you are the child with nuclear nightmares,
you know and suffer our human condition.

We know that nothing can separate us from your
love.

We pray for your love to enfold us in comfort,
your love to share our agony,
your love to inspire us to love one another,
your love to live in hope.

54 *Prayer for Lesbian and Gay People*

Gracious God,
We pray for gays and lesbians
who often face the fears and prejudices of a hostile
world
and church.

We pray for lesbians and gays
who often face discrimination in the workplace,
marketplace,
and in the place of worship.

We pray for gays and lesbians
who often face the risk of being outed, hunted,
shunned, shamed, shouted and preached at.

We pray for lesbians and gays
who often face for good or ill dubious findings
in science, politics, social research, and theology.

We pray for lesbians and gays
who often dare to bring a range of gifts
and the courage to be themselves into the community of the Way.

55 *At a Wedding*

God is love,
and those who live in love
live in God.

Love-giving God,
who created us in your image,
who walked with us in a garden,
heard our laughter, our quarrels,
promised us heirs and a community of hope;
God who brought us forth,
nurtured and fed us,
taught us to walk and run and grow,
made us for each other,
let your love surround and lead
(name) and *(name)* today and always.

Love-making Christ—
Carpenter, Teacher, Friend—
who changed water into wine at weddings,
cracked jokes about camels,
and took upon yourself the heavy yoke
of the world's sins:
Christ alive—in our lives,
in our community,
in our world—
let your love embrace and reconcile
(name) and *(name)* today and always.

Loving Spirit,
whose breath soft as butterfly wings
can move mountains,

whose fire can cleanse and renew;
Spirit, vibrant with joy and peace,
let your love comfort and challenge
(name) and *(name)* today and always.

56 *Lord of Weddings*

Lord of weddings where the ordinary took on
an extra special flavor,
May *(name)* and *(name)* taste the rich wine of
your love.
Let their love be a
listening
forgiving
honest
caring
sharing
of delight and chores
of good times and bad.
May they go out now with confidence
into the community as a new creation.
Lovers—made in your image.

57 *For Mourners*

Let us pray for those who mourn:

God, loving *(name)*
nearer to us than our next breath,
be with those who mourn.
Be in their shock, their grief,
their anger and despair

that they may grieve,
but not as those without hope.

Forgive all the harm they/we feel
they/we have done to *(name)*
and show them that they/we are forgiven.

We offer to you
all the regrets
the memories
the pain
the *if onlys,*
knowing that you
will surround those we mourn
with your presence
and heal them and us
of all that harms us.

58 *Prayers for a Funeral*

In the silence of our hearts
we bring before God *(name)*
to thank God for her/his whole life
and to remember her/him.

We remember *(name)* as a child and young adult
(add details of parents, siblings, place, etc.)

Silence

We remember *(name)* making his/her way in the
world,
especially *(add details of work, family, public life)*

Silence

We remember *(name's)* enjoyment of *(add interests, pursuits)*
and his/her skills at *(add skills, accomplishments)*

Silence

And we remember and give thanks for all *(name)*
was—his/her *(strength/warmth/courage/care for others or other attributes of personality)*

Silence

As we remember and give thanks for *(name's)* life,
so we also remember ourselves,
and we bring to God our sorrow, our sense of loss,
our grief.

Silence

And we bring to God the harder feelings we may have
over this death.
Help us to forgive any hurt *(name)* has caused us
and forgive us for any hurt we may have caused
(name).

Silence

God who holds us all with arms of love and
compassion
knows all we feel and endure at this time
and accepts and invites us to lean upon these
arms,
through Jesus Christ our Lord.

59 *After a Bereavement*

God of all life,
when all there is in our lives

is the empty space where the beloved was
and nothing can fill it
and we want nothing to fill it
because nothing, and no one, can take the place
of the beloved,
and we walk drearily through the days,
dragging one foot after the other,
and there is no joy in anything,
give us your strength in our sorrow,
your presence in the absence we feel,
your rest, that we may rise again to new life,
and your hope, that in death we are not divided.

God of all life,
when your people are mourning,
make us patient listeners
to the memories of happy times,
make us sensitive caregivers
so that we support but do not weaken,
make us good friends
so that we can hold the future open
for when our friends are ready to face it,
and hear our prayers for those recently bereaved...

| 60 | *Surrounded by a Cloud of Witnesses*

Each occasion
we glimpse them:
that turn of a head,
that smile,
the way she walked,
his sense of humor,

each time
a knife turns
in our heart.
In time,
through the windows of our tears
we see them
and smile.
In time,
we let go of sorrow.
In time,
beauty and music,
remembered places
bring solace not pain.
In your time,
God of all time,
may what we have sown in pain
be reaped in joy.

61 *Communion of Saints*

God of grace,
we thank you for the saints whom we ourselves
have known and loved.
It does not come easily to us to call them saints;
it seems as if ordinary mortals
are not good or great enough.
But you have given your people this name
and invited us into your company,
and you know how much we loved them.
So for these good companions,
whom we name before you for their love,
and for our love of them,
we give you grateful thanks *(names...)*

In the mystery of your love,
in the power of your spirit,
we are one with them.
We give great thanks.

62 *As You Love Yourself*

We pray for those who do not love themselves,
who cannot face the turmoil in their souls,
who put themselves down and call it selflessness,
who make themselves ill with bitterness,
who become sick with self-loathing.
Restore them and help them to live with
themselves
that they may joyfully live with each other.
And we pray for ourselves,
for the times when "they" include us.

63 *Prayer for Prophets*

Almighty God,
in whose prophets through the ages
we have seen your truth clearly outlined,
we pray for people of vision in our day:
those who carry undimmed
the light of the longing for justice;
those who speak in the councils of nations
to persuade and convince;
those who lead and support in action groups,
political parties, and networks;
those who resist blind power and risk persecution
to show a new way.

We pray for people in the front line of change—
newspaper editors, politicians, poets,
and people who are called to explore a common
future—
for prophets of speech and pen, canvas and lens,
for artists who are not afraid to look
and tell what they see,
who name what is deadly
and call us to new birth,
who trust their imagination
so that we may live life to the full.

LITANIES AND RESPONSES

64 *As Winter Trees*

As winter trees
stretch out bare arms to a dark sky,
WE STRETCH OUT IN THE DARKNESS
TO FIND THE TOUCH OF LOVE.

As snowdrops
turn their gentle faces to the sun,
WE LONG TO FIND IN THAT WARMTH
THE PROMISE OF PEACE.

As the fire
breaks the shell of the seed,
SO MAY OUR PAIN BREAK THE SHELL OF ISOLA-
TION THAT PROTECTS US FROM OURSELVES.

In the security of darkness,
the warmth of sunshine,
the promise of fire,
MAY WE BLOSSOM ANEW
IN THE MIRACLE OF YOUR SAVING LOVE,
O GOD.

65 *Wellspring of Our Lives*

Creator Spirit, wellspring of our lives,
as the refreshing rain falls on the just and unjust
alike,
REFRESH US WITH YOUR MERCY, WHO KNOW
OUR OWN INJUSTICE.

As a stream flows steadily on, defying all the odds
of stone and water,
FLOW OVER EVERY BOUNDARY AND BORDER
THAT SEPARATES US FROM EACH OTHER.

As the waters of our baptism washed us and wel-
comed us,
RENEW US NOW IN NEWNESS OF LIFE AND
UNITY OF LOVE.

As we were once held in the waters of our mother's
womb,
HOLD US IN THE POWER AND PEACE OF YOUR
ABIDING PRESENCE.

66 *Responses for a Burial*

Into the darkness and warmth of the earth,
WE LAY YOU DOWN.

Into the sadness and smiles of our memories,
WE LAY YOU DOWN.

Into the cycle of living and dying and rising again,
WE LAY YOU DOWN.

May you rest in peace, in fulfillment, in loving.
MAY YOU RUN STRAIGHT HOME INTO GOD'S
EMBRACE.[1]

---

[1]*A Book of a Thousand Prayers,* edited by A. Ashwin, HarperCollins
Publishers, 1996.

67 *Responses for a Cremation*

Into the freedom of wind and sunshine,
WE LET YOU GO.

Into the dance of the stars and the planets,
WE LET YOU GO.

Into the wind's breath and the hands of the star-maker,
WE LET YOU GO.

We love you, we miss you, we want you to be happy.
GO SAFELY, GO DANCING, GO RUNNING HOME.[2]

68 *God's Wisdom*

Lord Jesus, Teacher,
this is what you want us to learn,
not the world's wisdom, but God's.
And so we pray,
awaken us to our need of you in our lives
AND YOU WILL GIVE US YOUR LIFE.

Move us with sorrow for the sorrow of the world,
AND YOU WILL MAKE US STRONG THROUGH
OUR TEARS.

---

[2]Ibid.

Give us the humility to admit our failures,
AND YOU WILL BRING TREASURE OUT OF
THEM.

Make us hungry for justice,
AND YOU WILL GIVE US FOOD THAT LASTS.

Help us to see others through your eyes,
AND YOU WILL SHOW US OURSELVES WITH
LOVE.

Show us how to practice what we preach,
AND WE WILL SEE GOD IN EVERYONE.

Support us in standing firm for truth, even when it
costs,
AND THE TRUTH WILL ALSO MAKE US FREE.

CURSINGS AND BLESSINGS

69 *How Terrible*

A: How terrible for us
when we ignore the presence of strangers.

B: How terrible for us
when the sick and the old remain lonely.

A: How terrible for us
when the little ones are hurt or ignored.

B: How terrible for us
when the prisoner is deemed beyond redemption or love.

A: How terrible for us
when we do not question laws
that reward the strong and put down the
weak.

B: How terrible for us
when we know what we should do,
and we walk the other way.

A and B: How terrible for us,
for we bring God's anger upon ourselves,
and we walk into outer darkness.

(Based on Matthew 25)

70 *Cursed Be*

Cursed be garbage in an open sewer,
Cursed be the barbed wire of camps,
Cursed be the gassing and maiming of children.

71 *May the Maker's Blessing Be Yours*

May the Maker's blessing be yours,
encircling you round
above you
within you.

May the angels' blessing be yours
and the joy of the saints
to inspire you
to cherish you.

May the Son's blessing be yours,
the wine and the water,
the bread and the stories
to feed you
to remind you.

May the Spirit's blessing be yours,
the wind, the fire,
the still small voice
to comfort you
to disturb you.

And may my own blessing be yours—
a blessing rooted in our common pilgrimage,
the blessing of a friend.

72 *Blessing and Laughter and Loving*

Blessing and laughter and loving be yours,
the love of a great God
who names you

and holds you
while the earth turns and the flowers grow
this day
this night
this moment
and forever.[1]

73 | *Bless to Us, O God*

Bless to us, O God,
the doors we open,
the thresholds we cross,
the roads that lie before us.
Go with us as we go
and welcome us home.

74 | *The Love of the Faithful Creator*

The love of the faithful Creator,
The peace of the wounded Healer,
The joy of the challenging Spirit,
The hope of the Three in One
surround and encourage you
today, tonight, and forever.

75 | *As You Have Been Fed*

As you have been fed at this table,
go to feed the hungry.

---

[1]From *A Book of a Thousand Prayers,* edited by A. Ashwin, Harper-Collins Publishers, 1996.

As you have been set free,
go to set free the imprisoned.
As you have received—give.
As you have heard—proclaim.
And the blessing that you have received
from Father, Son, and Holy Spirit
be always with you.

76 *As You Were*

As you were in the ebb and flow,
as the beginning becomes the ending,
and the ending a new beginning,
be with us,
ever-present God.

77 *Wherever We Go*

Wherever we go,
may the joy of God the gracious
be with us.
Wherever we go,
may the face of Christ the kindly
be with us.
Wherever we go,
may the compassing of the Spirit of grace
be with us.
Wherever we go,
the presence of the Trinity around us
to bless and to keep us.

78 *We Have Laid Our Burdens Down*

We have laid our burdens down
in the presence of the living God.
We have been nourished for our journey
in the presence of the living God.
We have taken on the armor of Christ
in the presence of the living God.
Now lead us, guide us, defend us,
as we go into your world
in your name and for your sake,
O loving, living God.

REFLECTIONS, READINGS, AND MEDITATIONS

79 *Walking on the Water*

Biblical reading: Matthew 14:22-33.
This monologue may be used as a reflection on the biblical reading in worship on the theme of faith, trust, and risk taking.

He'd told us to cross the lake—
to go on home in the boat
and to leave him with the crowd on the shore.

I'd not wanted to do that.
We were, after all, his protectors;
without us there, who was to stop the people staying
with him all night,
wearing him out, demanding of him
more stories and cures and miracles?
But he'd insisted,
and given us no choice.
I'd no idea how he was intending to get home—
it was a long walk, and a lonely one.
It turned into a bad night.
A storm blew up—
it came out of nowhere,
and we were sailing straight into it.

The waves slapped against the sides of the boat,
the cold spray showering over us,
soaking us to the skin.
It was a night of nightmares.

And then the screams—
someone shouted out that they could see a man

walking toward us through the water—
a ghost,
a trick of the moonlight,
the spirit of a long-drowned sailor,
our imaginations ran riot.

And then a voice came out of the darkness,
a human voice,
a voice we knew
shouting through the storm—
"Have courage, it's me, don't be afraid."

There was a silence then, a strange silence,
as if the waves were waiting to see how we would
answer.

I heard myself speaking.
"Master, if it is you,
if it's really you,
tell me to come to you across the water."

Another silence,
and then a single word—
a word that filled me with terror and delight—
"Come."
I climbed over the boat's side,
and I walked toward him.
I felt like a child again,
balancing dangerously along the top of a high
wall,
full of laughter and of pride.
I had nearly reached him

when I felt the wind pulling at me,
buffeting me,
and I looked around me into the darkness,
and I panicked, and I sank,
splashing and spluttering into the cold waves.

At once he had hold of me,
telling me to trust him,
carrying me back to the boat.

I remember lying there,
curled up on the deck,
catching my breath,
clutching at the wet mast,
still feeling the strength of his body close to mine.

The wind had dropped by then,
and the others were sitting at his feet,
hardly able to look up at him.
One of them, trying to make sense of it all,
told him that he must be God's son.
He did not reply.
As we sailed eastward,
toward the dawning light,
the waves rocked us gently,
reassuringly,
as if God's hand were cradling us,
strengthening us,
soothing away our fears.

80   *If You Want To*

A man suffering from a dreaded skin disease came to Jesus, knelt down, and begged him for help. "If you want to," he said, "you can make me clean." Jesus was filled with pity, and reached out and touched him. "I do want to," he answered. "Be clean." At once the disease left the man, and he was clean. (Mark 1:40–43, TEV)

"If you want to."
Of course Jesus wanted to,
for his prayers and his actions were rooted in love,
the love of God
that set him free to be vulnerable and to care and
to live.

Of course he wanted to.
Love always wants the best for other people,
be they lepers,
mothers-in-law, strangers, or friends,
love always wants their lives to be whole and glad
and free.

And of course he wants us to.
For in our streets and communities
it is our hearts and lives he uses
to make his love and his healing and his justice
real.
It is through how we live and what we do
that good news and good things come to other
people.
And today he wants us to.
For he is here among us,

and it is our hands and our prayers
through which he comes to us and to those we
pray for.
And it is his love,
born and alive in us,
that will heal us and set us free.

81 *The Outsiders*

Appropriate biblical references may be used.

Voice 1:   I am not respectable—
           a single parent
           bringing the burden
           and blessing of my children
           into the presence of the disciples,
           those gray-suited men
           who are, of course,
           uniformly respectable.

Voice 2:   I am not respectable—
           I handle money,
           I get my hands dirty,
           I don't always get it right.
           Am I accountable?
           Whom do I really serve?
           People feel cheated by the system.
           I am part of the system.
           I am only human—
           and I handle money.

Voice 3:   I am not respectable—
           a woman of a certain age

with womb problems.
Period.
I'm not good company
(hysteria, you say)
intense, sometimes distressed,
disconcerting, undermining
your sense of what is decent and godly:
unclean.

Voice 4:   I am not respectable—
I have an illness
you would rather not mention,
never mind touch
with your tidy lives.
How did I get into this mess?
Whose fault was it?
Why do I persist
in calling attention to myself
and believing in healing?

Voice 5:   I am not respectable—
I was caught in the act.
They have all abandoned me:
my husband,
my lover—
I am alone
and ashamed.
I am at the mercy
of the righteous people
whose clean hands are full of stones.

Voices 1-5: We are not respectable—
we are poor, unemployed,

ill, in the wrong,
old, outsiders.
How did we come to be among you?
How can we expect your awareness,
never mind your acceptance?

Voice 1:   We are not respectable—
and yet we are welcomed
by Jesus,
who turns to listen to our voices,
who reaches out
to touch us
with hands he is not afraid to get dirty,
to embrace us;
who, in the moment of accepting us
for who we are,
shows us that we are forgiven
and worthy of respect.

82 *Nunc Dimittis*

May be used as a lead-in meditation for the Nunc Dimittis.
Biblical reading: Luke 2:22-38

It happened that
an old man and an old woman saw a word one
day
a word that looked familiar—
a word they thought they had seen many times
before,
an insignificant word and one of many like it
that had passed in front of their eyes that day.

Not a word to write home about,
not even a particularly well-presented word,
and probably not a word you'd find in better
circles—
just a rather scruffy word wrapped up in a small
cloth parcel.

But as they looked
a curious thing happened.
They knew that this was the word
that they had been waiting for all these years,
they knew that this was the word
that might fill the world with new talk,
they knew that this was the word
that would make sense of all words
they didn't know how they knew—they just
knew!

After they had managed
to catch their breath from surprise,
the old woman rushed out to tell anyone
who cared to listen about the word she had seen.
She sang a song about how this word
would change everything.

The old man held the word
in his tired but trembling hands,
and he also sang a song from the top of his
heart.

The word was brought to the temple
by Mary and Joseph.

The old woman was Anna—
the prophetess in the temple.
The old man was Simeon,
whose song we now say/sing together:

Lord now let your servant go in peace...

83 | *Yorkhill and Yarrows*

Our fourth child, Colin, was born with a harelip and cleft palate. When he was about nine months old, he went into Yorkhill Children's Hospital in Glasgow for an operation on his lip.

He had his operation on a Monday morning; on Tuesday, the wee soul looked as though he'd had a fight with Frank Bruno. I still remember his accusing eyes, how, even puffed-up and half-closed, they managed to convey his bewilderment and offense. It was almost as though he were asking, "Why are you letting this happen to me? Why am I suffering? Why don't you do something, Daddy?"

And it's so hard to take, for no matter how much you love the child, you are impotent to answer or take away the pain.

As I left the hospital that morning, I found myself thinking about the offense of life; thinking of the vast numbers of my sister and brother human beings for whom life is an offensive puzzle. The suffering children of Africa sprang immediately to mind, as do the many suffering children around the world today.

To the humiliated, the abused, and the oppressed of the world, surely life is an offense—and that cannot be God's will, cannot be the will of the God whose demand for justice is like a drumbeat running right through the Bible.

As I left the hospital that Tuesday morning, despite my discomfort at being unable to do anything for Colin, I was full of admiration for the surgeon's skill, the nurses' care, and the dedicated and cheerful work of the myriad of ancillary workers. My mind boggled, and still boggles, at the array of magical and wonderful tools of the healing people: the X-ray machines, the dialysis machines, the lasers, the microscopes, even the humble drips that are so often, literally, life-givers. The fruits of our modern technology.

I left Yorkhill Hospital that Tuesday morning to go to Yarrows, the famous warship builders on the River Clyde, where I was the industrial chaplain. Here was another community of people, men and women whose incredible skills, imagination, and inventiveness were every bit as wonderful as those of the hospital. From being among the hospital workers, nurses, and doctors who make up a community of healing, I was now among a community of workers whose great skills were being used to create the tools of death—for sadly, that's what warships are, and once we've built them, the best we can hope for is that they will never be used.

The contrast between what we ask decent, hardworking folk to do at Yorkhill and Yarrows struck me so clearly that day—and has never left me.

"The war to end all wars" has been fought, and still from here to the furthest-flung corners of the globe, the clamor for more and more, and better and better arms continues unabated. The dream of creating "a land fit for heroes" has been dreamt, and still old men sleep under railway arches, children are abused, women despair. When will we ever learn?

The great prophets of old consistently told of the fate of those who put their trust in chariots. They were doomed.

We do well to listen to the ancient word:

"Do you not know? Have you not heard?
The Lord is the everlasting God:
he created all the world.
He never grows tired or weary.
No one understands his thoughts.
He strengthens those who are weak and tired.
Even those who are young grow weak;
young men fall exhausted.
But those who trust in the Lord for help
will find their strength renewed.
They shall rise on wings like eagles;
they will run and not get weary;
they will walk and not grow weak."

This is the word of the Lord. We do well to listen.

I attended the launch of a Type 22 Frigate, the last of its kind, HMS Cumberland. She was launched by the Princess of Wales. Intoning the traditional words, "I name this ship Cumberland. May God bless her and all who sail in her," she cracked the bottle of champagne on the magnificent bow. The shipwrights down below knocked away the crucial stocks, and slowly at first, but quickly gathering momentum, she slid into the water, the environment for which she was created.

When the time came for her finally to leave the yard, she sailed down the river, a magnificent and awesome sight, armed to the teeth with all the latest and most sophisticated weapons that modern technology can produce. There was no denying her beauty, nor the pride in the building of her, yet the best that we could hope for was that she should never fire her mighty guns in anger; that one day she would go to the scrapyard with every missile on board still in its silo.

84 *Women at the Riverside*

Exodus 2:1-11

A: I am a Levite woman,
wife of a Levite man.
I carried his child
safe in the secret cradle of my womb
for nine months, afloat
in the waters of life,
until the day the waters broke
and he swam out into a dangerous world.
For three more months I hid him in our hut,
but his little voice grew stronger,
so one day I took a basket
woven of rushes that grow at the water's edge,
I daubed on tar to make it watertight,
a little coracle, then took it down
to float where the river lapped among the reeds.

B: I am his sister,
a small solemn child
standing by the side of a big river
to see what will happen.
I see the river, wide, lazy, slow-moving, life-bearing,
with the sun glinting on its smooth surface.
I cannot see our little cradle-boat
but I know it is there, hidden among the whispering reeds
with my baby brother.
I am a big sister, with a huge responsibility.
I see strangers coming down to the beach
to play, as though they haven't a care in the world,
to bathe in the river.

I see a great lady, one of our enemies.
Can she see the baby? What will she do?
My legs turn to water;
my eyes fill with tears.

C: I am Pharaoh's daughter.
I left the stale air of the palace,
the baking courtyards and colonnades,
the passions of politics,
the hard facts of life, the reasons of state.
I walked with my women
on the bare earth,
down to where the river offers
another way of being,
with its cool flow, its gentle caress, its feelings.
I wanted freedom to be myself
in another element,
and I fell for a baby.

D: I am a slave girl.
All I did was wade in deep
and fetch an ordinary basket
from where it was hidden in the rough reeds.
Did I guess its secret?
What did I feel,
as I held it, trembling,
and heard the hungry cries?
Who hears my voice?

C: I was moved with pity
by the tears of the baby.
I knew it must be a Hebrew child,

and suddenly, there at my elbow,
was another child:
not asking for money
like your normal urchin, but offering help:
"Do you want a nurse for the baby?"
The child has sense—a wise child.
I suspect there's more in this than meets the eye:
a story I don't know, an alien experience,
a strange and powerful torrent of feeling.
I accepted her help.

B: I called my mother, like a stranger.
A: I came and nursed my child, who knew me.
D: I found him, as lost as myself.
C: I adopted him, and called him Moses
because I drew him out of the water.

A: We are the women: a wife
B: A sister
C: A daughter
D: A slave—
women without names
All: But we are the ones
who trusted the child
to the strange and saving waters
and drew him out alive
and called him by name.

Author Index for Liturgies:

Author Index for Resources:

Index of Songs

EOA	JESUS CHRIST IS WAITING
PPPP	JUST AS A LOST AND THIRSTY DEER
CAYP	KUMBAYA
CAYP	LET THE GIVING OF THANKS
PPPP	LIFTING MY EYES UP TO THE HILLS
LFB	LISTEN, LORD
HSNW	LORD JESUS CHRIST, LOVER OF ALL
MAG	MAY GOD DRAW NEAR
PPPP	MAY THE WORDS OF OUR MOUTHS
PPPP	MY SHEPHERD IS THE LORD
EOA	NO ONE WILL EVER BE THE SAME
EOA	O BLESS THE LORD
PPPP	O GOD, YOU ARE MY GOD ALONE
CAYP	POUR OUT, I WILL POUR OUT
CAYP	SEND OUT YOUR LIGHT, LORD
SBTL	SENT BY THE LORD
PPPP	SING TO GOD WITH JOY AND GLADNESS
MAG	STAND FIRM
LFB	TAKE THIS MOMENT, SIGN AND SPACE
LFB	THE GOD OF HEAVEN
EOA	THE LOVE OF GOD COMES CLOSE
ILS	THE REFUGEES
HSNW	THE SONG IS LOVE
HSNW	THE STRANGEST OF SAINTS
HSNW	THE TEMPTATIONS
EOA	TRAVELING THE ROAD TO FREEDOM
EOA	VENI SANCTE SPIRITUS
FIC	WE ARE MARCHING IN THE LIGHT OF GOD
LFB	WE CANNOT MEASURE HOW YOU HEAL
HSNW	WHEN OUR LORD WALKED THE EARTH
CAYP	WORD OF THE FATHER

Key:

HSNW   HEAVEN SHALL NOT WAIT (Wild Goose Songs, vol. 1)

EOA   ENEMY OF APATHY (Wild Goose Songs, vol. 2)

LFB   LOVE FROM BELOW (Wild Goose Songs, vol. 3)

PPPP   PSALMS OF PATIENCE, PROTEST, AND PRAISE, by John L. Bell

CAYP   COME ALL YOU PEOPLE: SHORTER SONGS FOR WORSHIP, by John L. Bell

ILS   INNKEEPERS AND LIGHT SLEEPERS: 17 NEW SONGS FOR CHRISTMAS, by John L. Bell

MAG   MANY AND GREAT: SONGS OF THE WORLD CHURCH (vol. 1)

SBTL   SENT BY THE LORD: SONGS OF THE WORLD CHURCH (vol. 2)

(All published by Wild Goose Publications, Glasgow.)

BE NOT AFRAID
BY THE WATERS OF BABYLON
FOR THE HEALING OF NATIONS
THOSE WHO WAIT ON THE LORD
UBI CARITAS (TAIZE)
WE LAY OUR BROKEN WORLD
(The above songs are not published by Wild Goose Publications, but are widely anthologized.)

O GOD, THOU ART THE FATHER
ALMIGHTY FATHER OF ALL THINGS THAT BE
From *The Church Hymnary,* 3rd edition, OUP 1973.

THE LOVE BURNING DEEP
From *Love Burning Deep,* by Kathy Galloway, SPCK
1993.

GOD GIVE US POWER
HALLELUJAH, WE SING YOUR PRAISES
IPHARADISI
From *Freedom Is Coming,* edited by Anders Nyberg,
published by Utryck, Uppsala, Sweden, and avail-
able in the UK from Wild Goose Publications.